CONTENTS

Chairman: L Crawford
Head of Molecular Virology Unit
Imperial Cancer Research Fund, London

Current Approaches

Modern Trends in Aetiology and Management of Cervical Intraepithelial Neoplasia

Edited by
A Singer & V J Harten-Ash

duphar
medical relations

First published 1990

ISBN 1 870678 22 2

Printed in Great Britain by
Henry Ling Ltd., at the Dorset Press, Dorchester, Dorset

EPIDEMIOLOGY

Dr J Cuzick
Head of Department of Mathematics
Statistics and Epidemiology
Imperial Cancer Research Fund, London

INTRODUCTION

The epidemiological method has established some basic facts about the causes of cervix cancer but many questions remain unanswered or only partially answered. It is clear that some venerally transmitted agent is important, most likely the human papilloma virus, but other factors are needed also. Details of causative mechanisms can only be discovered by laboratory studies but epidemiology can give useful pointers as to what needs to be studied, and provides a useful perspective on the disease as a whole.

INTERNATIONAL VARIATION

International variations in cervical cancer rates are large. There is a tenfold difference between the high rates found in Cali-Columbia and other parts of South America and the low rates found in Israel and Spain. The reasons for these variations are not completely known and this has aroused much interest. It has been conjectured that these differences could be explained by the variation in prevalence of papilloma virus infections. However, biopsy specimens from India, Hong Kong and Singapore have shown lower rates of HPV in cervical cancers than have been found in western Europe, which is the reverse of that expected.

Incidence rates for cervical cancer are dropping throughout most parts of the world, particularly in Scandinavia, where there have been good screening programmes. Sadly, one of the exceptions to this has been England and Wales, where the rates have been virtually constant for the past 30 years, although some small changes are now being observed (Figure 1). For women of 55 years or above the rates of cervical cancer have remained largely unchanged. In the age group 45 to 54 years there has been a dramatic fall from around 400 cases per million per year to 200 cases. This is probably due to the limited success of the screening programme.

The worrying trend is that of younger women—the 25 to 34 age group, where large increases in incidence are occurring (Figure 1); giving a level of 180 cases per million per year in 1984. This is a cause of concern because in the past when the rates have been high in young women, those rates have been carried throughout their whole life. If this is a true increase, almost fourfold in 20 years, it is dramatic and frightening. There may be some over-diagnosis, however, as these are incidence rates not mortality rates. Pathologists are now

1

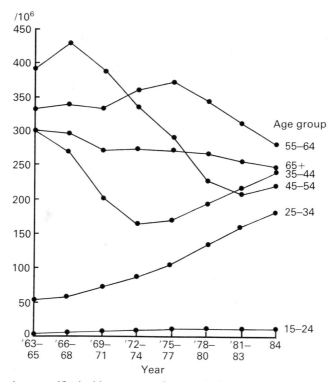

Figure 1. Age specific incidence rates for cervical cancer in England and Wales 1963–1984.

being much more careful about diagnosing micro-invasive disease particularly in younger women. The fact that the mortality rates are also going up in young women, however, is a reason to believe that this is not simply a diagnostic artefact but we are, in fact, in an era in which cervical cancer is becoming more common.

Valerie Beral[1] has made some cautious predictions about future rates and forecast that the number of cervix cancers in the under 50s is going to increase from 1500 to about 4000 by the year 2000. If one believes in a cohort effect then this increase will carry on beyond that, as women in their 20s now will be in their 30s and 40s in the year 2000, and most of the invasive cervical cancer will show up in their 40s and 50s. So the projections are for larger increases beyond the year 2000.

CERVICAL SCREENING

Cervical screening, when performed properly, provides much relative protection against invasive disease. In a large international study screening histories of women that develop cervical cancer have been compared to those women

2

TABLE 1. Geometric mean relative protection against cervical cancer in women with two or more previously negative smears participating in centrally organised screening programmes

Months since last negative smear	Relative protection (No. of cases)	95% Confidence limits
0–11	15.3 (25)	10.0 to 22.6
12–23	11.9 (23)	7.5 to 18.3
24–35	8.0 (25)	5.2 to 11.8
36–47	5.3 (30)	3.6 to 7.6
48–59	2.8 (30)	1.9 to 4.0
60–71	3.6 (16)	2.1 to 5.9
72–119	1.6 (6)	0.6 to 3.5
120+	0.8* (7)	0.3 to 1.6
Never screened	1.0	

*Based on figures from Aberdeen and Iceland only.

IARC (BMJ, 1986)[2]

who do not[2] (Table 1). If it is assumed that the screening programme functions correctly, with all women being screened when they should be and abnormal smears being correctly acted upon, it can be shown that the protection in the year following a second or subsequent negative smear is enormous, by a factor of 15. In the second year there is a twelvefold reduction in cancer rate and in the third year an eightfold one. In the fourth and fifth years the rate of protection rapidly drops to two to threefold rates compared to women that have never been screened. These data indicate that the three yearly screening is an effective procedure if the coverage is high enough, and that there are disadvantages to performing the screen every five years.

RISK FACTORS

The evidence is overwhelming that sexual activity is a prime factor. The variables that have been studied include the number of sexual partners of the women, the age of first intercourse and the behaviour of the individual males that are the sexual partners. These variables point to the human papilloma virus as being a major factor. Some studies have indicated that the age of first intercourse appears to be independent from and possibly as important than the number of sexual partners. It is difficult to be certain about this because the age at which sexual activity starts is related to the number of sexual partners. Rotkin[3] showed that the relative risk of subsequent cervical cancer was increased by a factor of over 10 following early sexual intercourse, which he took as under 15 years of age when compared to women with first intercourse after age 26 (Table 2).

TABLE 2. Relative risk and age at first intercourse

Age (years)	<15	15–17	18–20	21–23	24–26	>26
CIN	4.58	5.64	2.65	2.14	0.75	1
Invasive	11.10	15.16	9.81	3.35	3.65	1

(Rotkin, 1967)[3]

TABLE 3. Relative risk, number of partners and age at first intercourse

| Age (years) | Number of sexual partners | | | | χ^2 (Trend) |
	0–1	2	3–5	6+	
21 + or never	1.00	2.42	7.09	6.44	20.2
19–20	0.81	1.93	15.04	12.89	33.2
17–18	1.40	5.09	5.98	10.03	15.8
<17	1.55	1.90	8.82	7.52	12.3
χ^2 (Trend)	1.00	0.13	0.01	0.02	

(Harris et al, 1980)[4]

Ruth Harris and colleagues in Oxford[4] studied the number of sexual partners and the age of first intercourse as separate factors (Table 3). They found that the number of sexual partners was an important risk factor no matter what the age of first intercourse but the reverse was not true (Table 2). This particular study was one of the first to look at these two variables together, but subsequent studies have not confirmed that age at first intercourse is a secondary factor.

This would suggest that it is not only a question of transmission of a venereal agent, presumably the papilloma virus, but also the fact that the young cervix is particularly susceptible to certain kinds of insults, and this may relate to hormonal or other factors. This is an area that is unclear and it is uncertain how epidemiological studies are actually going to resolve this directly because of the close correlation between the age of first intercourse and the number of partners. This is an important question where other lines of research might be more illuminating.

In a classic study from Oxford, Buckley[5] looked at male behaviour and the number of sexual partners of husbands of women who developed cervical cancer, where the woman herself reported she had had only one sexual partner, that is, her husband (Table 4). The women were interviewed first and then a few years later, a male interviewer, completely separate from the original

4

TABLE 4. Male behaviour

| | Number of partners of husband | | | |
	1	2–5	6–15	>15
CIN	1.00	2.13	2.74	9.84
Invasive disease	1.00	1.65	2.63	7.82

Relative risk in women who reported only one sexual partner.

(Buckley et al, 1981)[5]

study, went back and interviewed the men as part of a general health study and asked him questions about his sexual behaviour, in a way that did not allow him to relate these results to the original interview. It was possible to show, even when women reported only one sexual partner, that the number of partners of the male was important in association with invasive disease or CIN lesions. This is confirmation of what you would expect when considering a venereally transmitted agent; if the husband has more than one partner he has more chance of picking up the agent and transmitting it to the woman.

Papilloma virus is present in many more cases than show even pre-invasive dysplastic changes. This has raised the question of co-factors and some of these are being studied actively both epidemiologically and in the laboratory. The factor that most stands out as requiring further attention is smoking because of the high risk of cervical cancer that has been found in the classic epidemiological studies. It has been known to be a risk factor for over 20 years but has been dismissed in a facile way as being simply another correlative of sexual behaviour—women that smoke tend to be more sexually active. The evidence that is now accumulating does not permit this kind of complacency to continue. Dr Barton is beginning to find some biological mechanisms which explain smoking as a possible risk factor and this is discussed in a separate chapter. Certainly the classical epidemiology gives every reason to believe that smoking is more than just a confounding variable and that it actually has something to do with the aetiology of this disease. Data from La Vecchia et al[6] on smoking showed clearly that the longer one smoked the greater the risk of cervical cancer (Table 5). Risk also depended on the amount smoked. He was

TABLE 5. Smoking and relative risk

| Invasive cancer | Non smokers | Current smokers Duration | | | | |
		<10	10–19	20–29	30–39	>40
Crude RR	1	1.09	0.99	1.36	1.71	3.63
Adjusted RR	1	1.27	0.95	1.39	1.51	7.82

(after La Vecchia et al, 1986)[6]

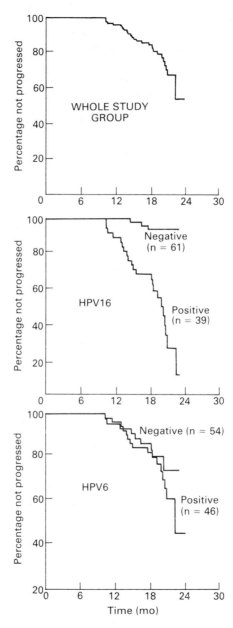

Figure 2. Percentage of patients showing disease progression to CIN III with time. First progression = 10 months.

(Campion *et al*, Lancet, 1986)[7]

6

also able to show that there is a relationship between smoking and the number of partners and that neither one of them individually explains the other. Together they produce even higher risks, than when viewed separately.

There has been a lot of concern about oral contraceptives acting as a co-factor. The evidence is very weak. They undoubtedly have a large indirect effect by allowing greater amounts of unprotected intercourse which allows, of course, veneral agent to be passed more freely.

Questions have arisen about diet. Primarily this data comes from the Third World where cervical cancer has been shown to be associated with dietary deficiencies of vitamins A and C. Studies that have looked at this in the Western World have not found any direct effect of diet. Vitamin A and C levels are normal in affected women. Diet is possibly a co-factor in some areas but does not seem important in Britain.

EPIDEMIOLOGY OF HUMAN PAPILLOMA VIRUS

The apparent importance of human papilloma virus in cervix cancer indicates that epidemiologic studies of prevalence of this virus and natural history studies of patients who are infected but otherwise normal will be useful. There are more than 40 different types of papilloma virus. The time progression from CIN 1 to CIN 3 has been studied where patients were followed by 4-monthly colposcopy and biopsied when there were signs of progression, Campion et al,[7] (Figure 2). Progression was correlated with the presence of HPV 6 or HPV 16 on the original smears that were taken. When HPV 6 results were analysed those that were negative progressed to CIN 3 at the same rate as those that were positive, a 50% progression in just under 2 years. However, vitually all of the women that had progressed had HPV 16. This was a highly significant difference adding a lot of weight to the theory that HPV 16 is important in the aetiology of cervical cancer in that, not only do you find it in invasive disease but that it also seems to be important in terms of predicting progression from mildly dysplastic lesions to severe dysplasia. At the moment the relevance of HPV 16 picked up in normal women is being studied. Dr Hollingworth at the Imperial Cancer Research Fund is doing a prospective study in which he is following up these women to see whether or not they develop CIN and what the co-factors are e.g. smoking. Prospective information will hopefully be available within another year.

REFERENCES

1 Beral V, Booth M. Predictions of cervical cancer incidence and mortality in England and Wales (letter). *Lancet* 1986;**ii**:495.
2 IARC Working Group on Evaluation of Cervical Cancer Screening Programmes. Screening for squamous cervical cancer: duration of low risk after negative results of cervical cytology and its implication for screening policies. *Br Med J* 1986;**293**:659–64.

3 Rotkin I D. Adolescent coitus and cervical cancer: associations of related events with increased risk. *Cancer Res* 1967;**27**:603–17.
4 Harris R W C, Brinton L A, Cowdell R H, Skegg D C G, Smith P G, Vessey M P, Doll R. Characteristics of women with dysplasia or carcinoma *in situ* of the cervix uteri. *Br J Cancer* 1980;**42**:359.
5 Buckley J D, Harris R W C, Doll R, Vessey M P, Williams P T. Case-control study of the husbands of women with dysplasia or carcinoma of the cervix uteri. *Lancet* 1981;**ii**:1010–4.
6 La Vecchia C, Franceschi S, Decarli A, Fasoli M, Gentile A, Parazzini F, Regallo M. Sexual factors, venereal diseases and the risk of intraepithelial and invasive cancer neoplasia. *Cancer* 1986;**58**:935–41.
7 Campion M J, Cuzick J, McCance D J, Singer A. Progressive potential of mild cervical atypia: prospective cytological, colposcopic, and virological study. *Lancet* 1986;**ii**:237–40.

DISCUSSION

Audience   What are the rates of HPV infection in normal women?

Dr Cuzick   This is the subject of Dr Hollingworth's study in which the data is actually being collected in North London at the moment. This data is not available for discussion at present but it is higher than was originally suspected. The Germans have done some prevalence studies of papilloma virus infection in sexually active women and found rates in the order of 30%.

Audience   Could you please elaborate on the risk in relation to diet?

Dr Cuzick   The primary evidence implicating diet directly comes from studies performed in India in which women with cervical cancer were compared to normal women and were interviewed about their diet. It was found that the former tended to have a lower consumption of leafy green vegetables, fresh fruits and foods high in vitamins C and A. Other evidence is rather indirect in that vitamin A, in particular, has been shown to be related to certain types of lung cancer and cervical cancer is also squamous cell. It was also used as a way of trying to explain why the rates were so high in some of the poorer parts of the world but that is very indirect.

Audience   Some of the early studies linked the incidence or the prevalence of cervical cancer with the socioeconomic status and/or occupation of the husband. There were certain occupations which apparently carried a higher risk for the wife. It was assumed that in these particular occupations the husbands had more sex partners, but in view of what you were saying about diet, would you like to comment on these observations.

Dr Cuzick   It is certainly true that there are particular occupations that have been associated with high risks of cervix cancer in wives, for example, long distance lorry drivers and coal miners. There are two explanations for this.

8

One is the sexual behaviour of long distance lorry drivers. In coal miners, for example, this is more difficult to explain but there is a suggestion that certain of the hydrocarbons in the dust might be carcinogenic and be sexually transmitted. These leads have not been followed up systematically and there is no good explanation. The other point of interest is that the social class gradient in cervical cancer is rapidly disappearing compared to 10 or 15 years ago when it was very much a lower class disease. In young women now, precancer shows no social class gradient whatsoever.

Audience If we had been sitting here 10 years ago another virus, herpes simplex, would have occupied our thoughts. I notice you do not even comment on this. Do you think that the considerable body of evidence linking HSV with cervical cancer can lightly be dismissed?

Dr Cuzick Yes.

Audience What evidence is there that chlamydia infection acts as a co-factor in CIN?

Dr Cuzick I have not personally been involved with these studies and the evidence is only suggestive. It is based on a theory that you need something more than papilloma virus and the possibility of chlamydia affecting the immune response of the cervix.

Audience You emphasised the fact that routine cervical screening every three years is adequate. Considering the high false negative rates which may result effectively in an adequate smear being taken only once in 6 years and recalling that some cases of CIN are aggressive, does this not mean that some invasive disease will be missed?

Dr Cuzick I think that is an important question which is difficult to answer. The rates of pre-invasive disease and invasive disease in young women have risen so much that it is not absolutely clear that 3 years is adequate in young women. National screening programmes need to be pragmatic. If one were to start 3 yearly screening at the beginning of sexual activity most women should have built up 2 to 3 negative smears before the age at which they are at all likely to have developed an invasive lesion. I think as a general principle that is probably adequate. One of the things that the screening programme really must do is to keep accurate records and to keep track of the results. If three years is then shown to be inadequate then there is a case for more screening particularly at younger ages.

A POSSIBLE ROLE FOR HUMAN PAPILLOMA VIRUS IN GENITAL CANCERS

Dr D McCance
Senior Lecturer in Microbiology
Guy's Campus, London

INTRODUCTION

The evidence for the association between the presence of HPV and various types of pre-invasive and malignant lesions of the cervix is well documented. HPV 16 and 18 account for 75–80% of the virus types that are found in invasive cervical cancer.

INTRACELLULAR CHANGES

There is a difference in the cellular interaction of the virus between pre-malignant and malignant cells. In a pre-malignant cell the virus is predominantly freely replicating and not associated with the chromosomes. It is producing infectious virus which can be detected. With invasive disease, the virus DNA becomes integrated into the chromosomes of the malignant cell. No longer is virus production occurring. In over 90% of tumours studied the virus has been integrated. The question is: 'Is that integration step essential for invasion or is it the consequence of some other cause of change in the cell'? This still remains to be answered, but the fact that integration is found so often suggests that it is not a chance event, and it may be one of the important steps in producing an invasive phenotype.

Karen Vousden's chapter discusses *in vitro* transformation studies, and it has been shown that rodent fibroblasts can be transformed with HPV 16 in collaboration with some oncogenes, of which *ras* has been the commonest. HPV 16 alone can also transform cells but at a reduced efficiency. So there must be a biological difference between the oncogenic potential of HPV 6, the virus associated with benign disease and a low grade CIN, and HPV 16 which is associated with all grades of CIN and invasive cancer. What is unknown is which part of the genome accounts for that difference.

Primary keratinocytes taken either from the foreskin or cervix can be studied while differentiating *in vitro*. Infection with HPV 16 inhibited this differentiation and it is possible to show that the abnormalities that develop are similar histologically to the abnormalities found in pre-malignant disease.

EXPERIMENTAL METHOD

Keratinocytes from the foreskin are grown in the laboratory like other cells. They are placed on top of a collagen gel, impregnated with 3T3 cells (mouse fibroblasts essentially for the keratinocytes growth). The gel is then placed on a raft (a stainless steel grid) and fed from underneath. Media percolates through the collagen gel and feeds the monolayer of cells on top. Within a few days there is a stratification of the cells as in a normal epithelium. Differentiation also occurs and can be shown by the fact that the upper cells produce differentiation-specific keratins at the air/liquid interface. This method of *in vitro* differentiation of keratinocytes was then used to observe how the introduction of HPV 16 virus might upset this differentiation. There are a number of different manipulations used to get the viral DNA into the cells. Keratinocytes are rather difficult and the best method was to pass a current through the media containing the cells and viral DNA. Once the viral DNA is incorporated into the cells the normal orderly stratification breaks down. There is disorganisation of the basement membrane and parabasal areas, and vacuolation of the cytoplasm, supposedly pathognomonic of HPV infection. The cells also become immortalised. Normally keratinocytes will only grow for about 50 cell generations. With the viral DNA integrated in them they grow forever. A cell line started in April 1987 has achieved over 1500 cell generations. It is also possible to show that the capacity for the cells to differentiate becomes less with increasing numbers of replications, eventually losing the ability totally. Mitotic figures start to develop in the upper part of the epithelium of raft cultures. There is a great reduction in the biochemical differentiation as well as the morphological inhibition. This is, of course, the picture seen in CIN 3 and therefore added evidence is given to a direct association of these viruses and CIN.

It is important to remember that not all cervices with HPV 16 infection develop such a loss of differentiation, pre-malignant change, and malignant transformation. It is probably that HPV infection sows the seed and many other factors are necessary for that seed to germinate into a malignant disease.

DISCUSSION

Mr Soutter   What sort of controls are you using in these experiments with keratinocytes? Obviously you are manipulating cells considerably in order to transfect them?

Dr McCance   Two controls. We have the DNA cloned into a bacterial plasma so we can grow it up in bacteria. We put in the plasma on its own and the cells die after the prerequisite time. In other words, they die like normal cells do. They senesce after 50 or so generations.

The other thing we have done is to put in another viral oncogene which has nothing to do with human cancer, but it can transform cells *in vitro*. This gene can immortalise the cell but without causing a lack of differentiation.

So on two counts we have controls: a plasma that does nothing to the cell but is part of the input DNA that we inserted, so it is obviously the HPV 16 that causes difference between the two; and in the other case immortalised cells caused by a separate viral agent where differentiation occurs. This means that there is probably something specific to HPV interacting with the cells, inhibiting its differentiation.

Audience   What happens if you put HPV 6 or 11 through this system?

Dr McCance   We do not know. We have just got cultures going now with HPV 6 in them. It is a long extrapolation from mouse fibroblasts to human keratinocytes but I think HPV 6 may do something, but it remains to be seen exactly what.

Audience   I find puzzling the fact that integrated DNA is not found in the early CIN lesions. It fits in nicely with your experimental data but it suggests strongly that there must be something else going on.

Dr McCance   I did qualify my statement by saying that the DNA seems predominantly to be non-integrated. In fact there are three published studies showing integrated DNA within pre-malignant disease. The reason I do not talk about them is that the blots are not that easy to interpret or could be interpreted in other ways. Also there are technical difficulties in detecting integration in pre-malignancy, since it probably occurs in only a minority of cells.

Dr Crawford   It is a difficult point, but there has been this very strong correlation between integration and progressive malignancy. It is hard to disprove that this is not simply an occurrence with time, and that integration itself is not an essential component. There is no evidence that the position into which the virus DNA integrates in the cellular genome has much importance because a great variety of adjacent sequences have been picked up. So the mechanism for transformation is not one which involves integration within a particular region or sequence. I think there are situations where you actually do get malignant fully transformed cells which still contain, at least the majority of the viral DNA non-integrated usually as polymers, but it is impossible in these circumstances to prove that there is nothing integrated and therefore it remains an open question.

CELLULAR TRANSFORMATION BY HUMAN PAPILLOMAVIRUS TYPE 16

Dr Karen Vousden
Senior Scientist
Ludwig Institute, London

INTRODUCTION

Previous chapters have shown that Human Papillomaviruses (HPVs), particularly HPV16, may be involved in the development of cervical carcinoma. It is possible that the expression of HPV16 gene products is involved in the conversion of normal to malignant cells. In order to test this hypothesis the transforming potential of HPV16 genes has been studied in cell culture systems. Following the introduction of HPV16 DNA into suitable recipient cells by the technique of transfection,[1] the effects of expression of viral sequences on the cells are analysed.

Papillomaviruses have small genomes which can be broadly divided into two regions; the late region containing the open reading frames which encode the viral structural proteins and the early region which contains open reading frames encoding proteins which presumably play a role during the early stages of viral infection. Some of these early region proteins may also play a role in malignant change. The viral DNA is normally maintained and replicated episomally in the host cell. However, in tumour cells the DNA is frequently found to be integrated into the host DNA.[2] The significance of this integration remains unclear, one consistent observation has been that the integration occurs so that two of the viral open reading frames, E6 and E7, remain uninterrupted and these proteins are expressed in tumour cells.[3,4] This may give an indication that the expression of E6 and E7 is important to the development and maintenance of the tumour, John Tidy will discuss this in more detail in the next chapter.

Assays to measure activity of HPV16 sequences *in vitro*

Recipient cells for transfection experiments can be divided into two main groups, established cell lines and primary cells. Most transfection studies have been carried out using rodent cells as recipients, although we are beginning to develop assays using human cells. The following discussion, however, considers experiments carried out in mouse or rat cells.

The established cell lines used have, for all practical purposes, an infinite life span in culture but remain otherwise untransformed. Such cells, which include NIH3T3, C127 and RAT-1 cells, can be used to test the transforming capacity of transfected DNA sequences. Indicators of transformation include loss of contact inhibition, morphological transformation, the acquisition of anchorage independence and the ability to form tumours in nude mice.

Primary cells such as rat embryo fibroblasts (REFs) or baby rat kidney cells (BRKs) have not been established in culture and so show a limited life span after which they stop dividing and senesce. These cells can be used to assay the immortalising activity of the transfected sequences. Immortalisation is either assayed by the ability of transfected cells to continue dividing beyond their normal life span, or by transformation when the potential immortalising sequences are co-transfected with a second oncogene, normally activated *ras*.

Transfection of established cells

The established mouse cell line NIH3T3 was used as a recipient for transfection with the HPV16 constructs shown in Figure 1. p16EXMo contains the entire early region, although the clone of HPV16 used here has an interruption in the E1 open reading frame.[5] P16NXMo contains only the E2, E4 and E5 open reading frames whereas in p16HHMo only E6 and E7 remain intact. In the two smallest constructs either only E6 (p16E6Mo) or E7 (p16E7Mo) can be fully expressed. Each of these regions of the HPV16 genome was placed under the control of a heterologous promoter, the Molony murine leukaemia virus long terminal repeat (MoLTR), which is very active in NIH3T3 cells. The cells were transfected and studied for evidence of transformation.[6]

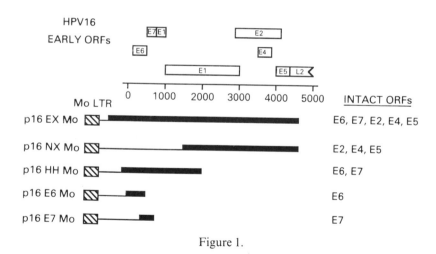

Figure 1.

Although cells transfected with the entire early region of HPV16 (p16EXMo) were not obviously morphologically transformed it was found that they had acquired the ability to grow into colonies in soft agar, they had become anchorage independent. Using the smaller constructs to localise this activity it was shown that the construct containing E6 and E7 (p16HHMo) behaved the same as the construct with the entire early region. However, cells transfected with E2, E4 and E5 sequences (p16NXMo) remained anchorage

14

dependent and were unable to grow in soft agar. Finally the two smallest constructs were used to determine whether E6 or E7 or both were required for the transformation of NIH3T3 cells. These experiments demonstrated that transfection with E7 sequences only (p16E7Mo) would induce anchorage independent growth whereas expression of E6 (p16E6Mo) could not transform these cells. These results were confirmed using a series of isogenic plasmids containing both E6 and E7 sequences (p16HHMo) but carrying a linker which introduced a premature termination mutation in one or other of the open reading frames. A construct carrying the stop codon in E6 but expressing full length E7 was able to transform NIH3T3 cells. When the termination mutation was introduced into E7 sequences (leaving E6 intact), no transformation was observed.

In summary, HPV16 sequences were shown to be capable of inducing anchorage independent growth of NIH3T3 cells and this activity could be localised to E7. Other studies have shown E7 to be transforming in other established cell lines.[7] The tranformation induced by E7 is only partial. The cells grow in soft agar but there is no obvious morphological transformation and the cells are not readily tumorigenic in nude mice. However, some recent studies have indicated that the expression of E6 contributes to the tumorigenicity of these cells.[8]

Transfection of primary cells

Previous studies have demonstrated that HPV16 sequences can cooperate with *ras* to transform BRK.[9] Again the principal activity in these studies was localised to E7. We have used a different assay for immortalisation using the tsa14 cell line which was developed by Parmjit Jat.[10] tsa14 cells were derived by infecting REFs with a retrovirus encoding a temperature sensitive SV40 large T antigen (LT). SV40 LT is a very potent immortalising gene. However, the temperature sensitivity of LT in tsa14 cells results in a cell line which is immortal at the permissive temperature (33°) but at the non-permissive temperature (39.5°), where LT is rapidly degraded, the cells stop dividing and senesce like primary cells. The introduction of wild type SV40 LT sequences or adenovirus E1a, another immortalising gene, can rescue tsa14 cells and allow continuous growth at the non-permissive temperature. Using the HPV16 constructs described in the last section, we were able to demonstrate that expression of E6 and E7 could rescue tsa14 cells at 39.5° but the construct containing E2, E4 and E5 had no detectable activity in this assay. In contrast to the results obtained using established cells, it was shown that E6 and E7 could independently immortalise these cells although the activity of E6 was significantly weaker than E7. Interestingly, another well established immortalising gene, *myc*, was shown to be unable to function in this assay.

Using the tsa14 cells an immortalising activity has been demonstrated for HPV16 E7 and, more weakly, for E6. This assay is able to distinguish two classes of immortalising genes, those which can rescue tsa14 cells at 39.5° (SV40 large T, adenovirus E1a and HPV16 E7) and those which cannot rescue

15

(*myc*). It is therefore evident that HPV16 E7 can functionally substitute for SV40LT and the results suggest that HPV16 E7, SV40 large T and adenovirus E1a immortalise cells by a common mechanism which is not shared by *myc*.

SUMMARY

Using experimental *in vitro* systems involving transfection of DNA into suitable recipient cell lines it has been demonstrated that HPV16 E7, and to a lesser extent E6, have both transforming activity in established cells and immortalising activity in primary cells. These results support the hypothesis that the expression of E6 and E7 play a role in the development and maintenance of cervical carcinomas.

REFERENCES

1 Wigler M, Pellicer A, Silverstein S, Axel R, Urlaub G, Chasin L. *Proc Natl Acad Sci USA* 1979;**76**:1373–6.
2 Durst M, Kleingeinz A, Hotz M, Gissmann L. *J Gen Virol* 1985;**66**:1515–52.
3 Baker C C, Phelps W C, Lindgren V, Braun M J, Gonda M A, Howley P M. *J Virol* 1987;**61**:962–71.
4 Schneider-Gadicke A, Schwarz E. *EMBO J* 1986;**5**:2285–92.
5 Durst M, Gissmann L, Ikenberg H, zur Hausen H. *Proc Natl Acad Sci USA* 1983;**80**:3812–5.
6 Vousden K H, Doniger J, DiPaolo J A, Lowy D R. *Oncogene Res* 1988;**3**:167–75.
7 Kanda T, Furono A, Yoshiike K. *J Virol* 1988;**62**:610–3.
8 Yutsudo M, Okamuto Y, Hakura A. *Virology* 1988;**166**:594–7.
9 Matlashewski G, Schneider J, Banks L, Jones N, Murray A, Crawford L. *EMBO J* 1987;**6**:1741–6.
10 Vousden K H, Jat P S. *Oncogene* 1989. In press.

HPV-DNA INTEGRATION AND GENE EXPRESSION

Dr John Tidy

Clinical Research Fellow

Ludwig Institute, London

INTRODUCTION

Over 50 different HPVs have now been typed and at least 8 types infect the female genital tract. The majority of invasive tumours of the cervix are associated with HPVs 16, 18 or 33.[1] In an infected cell the HPV DNA is located within the nucleus and may exist in two different physical states. The HPV DNA may be present either as free circles, called episomes, which are separate from the cellular DNA or the HPV DNA may become integrated into the cellular DNA. The mechanism by which episomal HPV is integrated into the host genome and the resulting alteration in both HPV and host cell gene expression may be of considerable importance in the neoplastic process. Integration of HPV DNA is probably an early event in the process since normal cervical tissue[2] and HPV-16 immortalised cell lines established from normal cervical tissue[3] contain integrated HPV sequences. Most invasive cervical tumours possess some integrated HPV-DNA sequences.[4] The sites at which HPV-DNA is integrated into the cellular DNA would appear to be random in nature and not linked to any specific cellular genes.[5] The study of cervical tumours and cell lines derived from cervical tumours suggests that while the upstream regulatory region (URR)-E6-E7 portion of the virus remains intact following integration the E1-E2 region may be disrupted by the selective opening of the episomal HPV within this region.[6,7]

Twenty three tumours from women undergoing surgery for stage IB carcinoma of the cervix were studied. The DNA was formally extracted from each tumour. Each tumour DNA was digested with several bacterial restriction enzymes and the fragments separated by gel electrophoresis. The DNA fragments were then transfered to filters by Southern blotting[8] and the filters subsequently hybridised with a radioactive HPV-16 probe. The filters were then exposed to X-ray film. The presence of HPV-16 DNA is indicated by a dark band on the X-ray film. All 23 tumours were positive for HPV-16. The pattern of bands produced using the various restriction enzymes indicated the presence of integrated or episomal HPV-16 sequences. Seven tumours contained only integrated HPV-16 DNA, nine contained episomal and integrated HPV-16 DNA and seven contained only episomal HPV-16 DNA. To determine if the URR-E6-E7 region of HPV-16 was selectively maintained intact while the E1-E2 region was interrupted as a consequence of integration the tumour DNAs were further studied. The restriction enzyme Pst I cuts episomal HPV-16 at five points releasing six fragments of different sizes. One

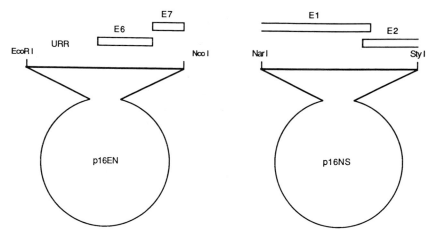

Figure 1. HPV16 subgenomic probes used to determine maintenance or interruption of open reading frames.

fragment (2.8 kb in length) encompasses the E1-E2 region and another fragment (1.8 kb in length) encompasses the URR-E6-E7 region. Two probes were constructed, p16NS which contains only the E1-E2 region and p16EN which contains only the URR-E6-E7 region (Figure 1). After digestion with Pst I each tumour was probed with p16NS and p16EN. The presence of fragments other than those predicted indicate that the region has been disrupted as a consequence of integration (Figures 2 and 3). There was evidence that the E1-E2 region was interrupted or had suffered a partial deletion in 13 of the 16 tumours containing integrated HPV-16. The URR-E6-E7 region was maintained intact in all the tumours studied.

When HPV-16 is integrated into the host genome it would appear that the episome is opened preferentially within the E1-E2 region while the URR-E6-E7 region is maintained intact. A consequence of this must be the restriction of HPV-16 gene expression, a phenomenon which has previously been reported.[9] The loss of E2 may also have considerable effect on early gene expression. The E2 protein, particularly in bovine papillomavirus, regulates early gene expression by binding to sites within the URR. Normally the E2 protein down regulates gene expression and so the loss of this protein, as a result of integration, may allow aberrant expression of the E6 and E7 proteins.[10-13]

Analysis of two tumours, both containing only episomal HPV-16, showed both to have a 1.4 kb fragment as well as the 1.8 kb fragment when probed with p16EN (Figure 3, lanes 3 and 4). Further analysis of the tumour DNAs with other restriction enzymes and smaller probes from within the URR-E6-E7 region revealed that the 400 bp deletion lay within the URR. To further map this deletion the polymerase chain reaction[14] was used to amplify both the wild type sequence and the deletion (ΔCR-16). The DNA sequence of ΔCR16 has a 325 bp deletion from position 7598 to 17 and a point mutation A to C is

18

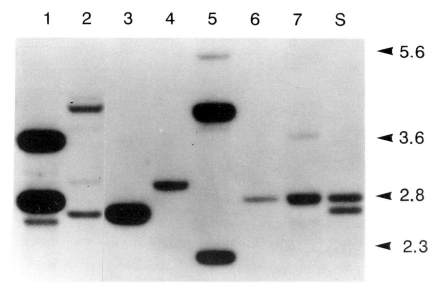

Figure 2. Southern blot of cervical carcinomas digested with the enzyme PstI and probed with p16NS.

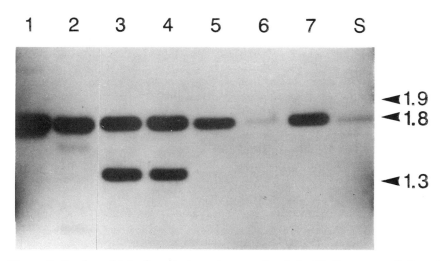

Figure 3. Southern blot of cervical carcinomas digested with the enzyme PstI and probed with p16EN.

also present at position 20 (Figure 4). The deletion and point mutation are the same in both tumours. The deletion removes the glucocorticoid responsive element and the keratinocyte core enhancer from the URR. The glucocorticoid responsive element has a positive effect on gene transcription in response

19

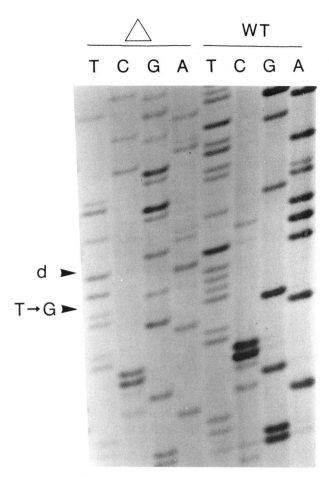

Figure 4. Sequencing gel of the antisense strand demonstrating the deletion (d) and the point mutation (T to G) in ΔCR16 compared with wild type HPV16.

to dexamethasone but the response to sex steroids is uncertain.[15] The keratinocyte enhancer responds to a uncharacterised factor present in keratinocytes which may explain the tissue trophism shown by this group of viruses.[10] The effect of the loss of these elements on early gene transcription is unknown. The contribution of ΔCR-16 to the neoplastic process has still to be evaluated.

HPV-16 DNA AND TUMOUR MAINTENANCE

If HPV-16 DNA is present in the primary tumour is it present in the metastatic deposits arising from the primary and so by implication required for the maintenance of the malignant phenotype?

Thirteen women undergoing radical hysterectomy for stage IB carcinoma of the cervix were studied. One hundred and thirty five lymph nodes were resected and a portion of each node analysed for HPV-16 DNA. The remainder of the lymph node was sent for histology. Ten women had squamous cell carcinoma and three had adenocarcinoma of the cervix. Metastatic deposits were found in 30% of cases. HPV-16 was present in six squamous cell tumours and one adenocarcinoma. One squamous cell carcinoma and two adenocarcinomas were positive for HPV-18.

Two unusual patterns emerged from analysing the lymph node DNA. Using Southern blotting one group of women, with HPV-16 positive primaries, had lymph nodes that were positive for HPV-16 yet there was no evidence of metastatic disease. In a second group of women only 50% of the metastatic deposits from HPV positive primaries had evidence of HPV DNA. Previous studies have reported the presence of HPV DNA in all metastatic deposits derived from HPV positive primaries.[16]

The polymerase chain reaction was used with the lymph node DNA to determine if the lack of HPV DNA in the metastatic lymph nodes was a reflection of the low sensitivity of Southern blotting. Using PCR all the metastatic lymph nodes were positive for HPV DNA. When the PCR method was applied to the disease free lymph nodes from women either with a HPV positive primary or an HPV infection of the vagina over 90% were positive for HPV DNA. It is currently unclear as to whether HPV sequences are present perhaps arising from micrometastases, or whether the HPV has been moved to the regional lymph nodes as part of the local immune response to the viral infection.

CONCLUSIONS

Integration of HPV DNA is probably an early event in cervical neoplasia. The selective opening of episomal HPV-16 within the E1-E2 will restrict the expression of the E2 protein which has an important role in regulating early gene expression. The expression of the transforming proteins, E6 and E7, may therefore be abnormal in these cells and may contribute to the oncogenic process. In tumours where there is only evidence of episomal HPV-16 the presence of variant forms of HPV, such as the one described may be of importance.

The increased sensitivity of PCR in detecting HPV DNA has shown that the virus may be present in the regional lymph nodes following infection in the absence of metastatic disease. The PCR technique will be of considerable value in ascertaining the true prevalence of HPV infection in the normal population.

REFERENCES

1 Tidy J A, Farrell P J. Viruses and cervical neoplasia. In: The Molecular Biology of Cancer (eds Waxman J and Sikora K) Blackwells Scientific Publications. Oxford, 1989; 101–17.

2 Murdoch J B, Cassidy L J, Fletcher K, Cordiner J W, MacNab J C M. Histological and cystological evidence of viral infection and human papillomavirus type 16 DNA sequences in cervical intraepithelial neoplasia and normal tissue in the west of Scotland: evaluation of treatment policy. *Brit Med J* 1988;**296**: 381–5.

3 Schneider-Maunoury S, Croissant O, Orth G. Integration of human papillomavirus type 16 DNA sequences: a possibly early event in the progression of genital tumours. *J Virol* 1987;**61**:3295–8.

4 Durst M, Kleinheinz A, Hotz M, Gissmann L. The physical state of human papillomavirus type 16 DNA in benign and malignant tumours. *J Gen Virol* 1985;**66**:1515–22.

5 Durst M, Croce C M, Gissmann L, Schwarz E, Huebner K. Papillomavirus sequences integrate near cellular oncogenes in some cervical carcinomas. *Proc Natl Acad Sci USA* 1987;**84**:1070–4.

6 Schwarz E, Fresse K B, Gissmann L, Mayer W, Roggenbuck B, Stremlau A, zur Hausen H. Structure and transcription of human papillomavirus sequences in cervical carcinoma cells. *Nature* 1985;**314**:111–4.

7 Choo K-B, Pan C-C, Han S-H. Integration of human papillomavirus type 16 into cellular DNA of cervical carcinoma: preferential deletion of the E2 gene and invariable retention of the long control region and the E6/E7 open reading frames. *Virology* 1987;**161**:259–61.

8 Southern E M. Detection of specific sequences among DNA fragments separated by gel electrophoresis. *J Mol Biol* 1975;**98**:503–17.

9 Shirasawa H, Tomita Y, Kubota K, Kasai T, Sekiya S, Takamizawa M, Simizu B. Transcriptional differences of the human papillomavirus type 16 genome between precancerous lesions and invasive carcinomas. *J Virol* 1988;**62**: 1022–7.

10 Cripe T P, Haugen T H, Turk J P, Tabatabai F, Schmid III P G, Durst M, Gissmann L, Roman A, Turek L P. Transcriptional regulation of the human papillomavirus-16 E6-E7 promoter by a keratinocyte-dependent enhancer, and by viral E2 trans-activator and repressor gene products: implications for cervical carcinogenesis. *EMBO J* 1987;**6**:3745–53.

11 Thierry F, Yaniv M. The BPV1-E2 transacting protein can either be an activator or a repressor of HPV18 regulatory region. *EMBO J* 1987;**6**:3391–7.

12 Moskaluk C A, Bastia D. Interaction of the bovine papillomavirus type 1. E2 transcriptional control protein with the viral enhancer: purification of the DNA-binding domain and analysis of its contact points with DNA. *J Virol* 1988;**62**:1925–31.

13 Dostatni N, Thierry F, Yaniv M. A dimer of BPV-1 E2 containing a protease resistant core interacts with its DNA target. *EMBO J* 1988;**7**:3807–16.

14 Saiki R K, Grelfand D M, Stoffel S, Scharf S J, Miguchi R, Horn G T, Mullis K B, Erlich H A. Primer directed en amplification of DNA with a thermostable DNA polymerase. *Science* 1988;**239**:487–91.

15 Gloss B, Bernard H U, Seedorf K, Klock G. The upstream regulatory region of the human papillomavirus type 16 contains an E2 protein independent enhancer which is specific for cervical carcinoma cells and regulated by glucocorticoid hormones. *EMBO J* 1987;**6**:3735–43.

16 Lancaster W D, Castellano C, Santos C, Delgado G, Kurman R J, Jenson A B. Human papillomavirus deoxyribonucleic acid in cervical carcinoma from primary and metastatic sites. *Am J Obstet Gynecol* 1986;**154**:115–9.

DISCUSSION

Dr Crawford   Where you locate HPV-16 DNA sequences in the lymph nodes, can you tell in which cell it is resident e.g. within lymphocytes, macrophages or within epithelial origin cells?

Dr Tidy   Not with the *in situ* hybridisation technique. It may be possible with the advent of the polymerase chain reaction.

Dr Crawford   It is certainly important to establish whether it is on its way out or moving on in an active form.

Dr Tidy   Yes indeed. If it is in an active form and perhaps linked to a cancer cell this may explain the group of women who relapse locally with invasive carcinoma at an early stage.

Dr Crawford   It is certainly true that HPV-16 DNA is more widespread than evidence would indicate. Later we shall consider what determines which of those cells with HPV DNA go on to become malignant.

Audience   Are you going to define the population in terms of their sexual partners? I think it is important to know whether HPV-16 exists within the genital tract of males and females who have been mutually exclusive as opposed to the general population.

Dr Tidy   No. I take your point, but at the moment we are performing only a feasibility study. That question certainly warrants consideration.

Audience   Does the finding of HPV-18 in adenocarcinoma indicate specificity?

Dr Tidy   Yes, in this study 50% of adenocarcinomas are associated with HPV-18 compared to 10% of squamous cell carcinomas. As adenocarcinoma constitutes only 10% of invasive carcinomas of the cervix, however, there is insufficient data available to draw serious conclusions.

Audience   Pathologically squamous cell carcinoma is often seen in association with adenocarcinoma. Do you get HPV-16 in both lesions?

Dr Tidy   I have not come across this. I do not know of any paper that has addressed this issue.

COFACTORS IN THE CAUSATION OF CERVICAL INTRAEPITHELIAL NEOPLASIA: POSSIBLE IMMUNOLOGICAL MECHANISMS OF ACTION

Mr S E Barton

Research Fellow in Gynaecology,

Whittington Hospital, London

INTRODUCTION

One currently popular hypothesis for the development of cervical neoplasia[1,2] proposes that epithelial infection by human papillomavirus (HPV) is an important precursor of premalignant and malignant transformation. In particular, HPV type 16 has been implicated in both cervical intraepithelial neoplasia (CIN)[3] and invasive disease.[4] However, the recent detection of this viral subtype in normal cervical epthelium[5] has been used to cast doubt on the role of HPV in the development of cervical neoplasia.[6] This is further complicated by the finding that in women with cervical HPV type 16 infection but normal cytological smears, colposcopic examination may reveal a significant number of CIN lesions.[7] Overall, it is clear that not all women with cervical HPV (even type 16) infection develop invasive disease. To explain this discrepancy, the role of various cofactors (e.g. cigarettes, oral contraceptives, semen, cervical infections) have been proposed although the exact mechanisms of action of these agents remains unknown.

The host immune response in cervical neoplasia

Immunocompromised women have been found to have an increased incidence of cervical neoplasia.[8,9] This clinical observation has led to increased interest in the role of the host immunology of the cervical epithelium in the development of cervical neoplasia. Using immunocytochemical techniques, the populations of immunologically significant cells in the normal cervix have been delineated in our laboratory at the Whittington Hospital. The results[10–13] have shown that in normal squamous cervical epithelium, Langerhans' cells are the most prominent antigen presenting cell with relatively few macrophages present. T lymphocytes are predominantly found in the region of the basement membrane, with individual subsets of T4 and T8 lymphocytes in proportions similar to the systemic circulation. B cells are rarely found in squamous cervical epithelium.

The changes in the local immunology of the cervical epithelium seen in HPV infection and CIN have also been investigated (Table 1). These include a decrease in Langerhans' cells[10] and a decreased T-cell count,[11] especially of the

TABLE 1. Changes in the local immune cell populations in HPV1/CIN[10-13]

—Decreased Langerhans' cell count.
—Decreased T cell count.
—Inverted T4/T8 ratio.
—Increased macrophage count.
—Stromal NK cell infiltration.
—No change in B cells.

T4 or helper subset. These changes represent a reduction in the cells which recognise and present viral antigens, as well as those which become activated by this process to respond to viral infection. This may constitute a state of localised immunosuppression in HPV infection, which seems to persist and worsen with increasingly severe grades of CIN. The functional significance of the observed macrophage[12] and natural killer cell[13] infiltrates into these CIN/HPV lesions is at present unknown.

In recent studies, we have investigated whether the HPV subtype or any of the cofactors postulated for the development of neoplasia, exert their effect by altering the local immune defences of the cervix.

Summary of 'Cofactors' Study

Women attending a community colposcopy clinic were studied. These included those with both prior normal and abnormal cervical cytology. Each woman had a full history taken, especially details of her smoking, contraception and any previous genital infections. Cervical cytology was repeated, a smear was taken for filter in situ hybridisation detection of HPV type 16 DNA, and endocervical swabs were taken to exclude common cervical infections.

Standard colposcopic examination was then performed, with directed biopsy of any abnormal area. In women without any abnormality, a representative biopsy of the transformation zone was obtained.

The biopsies were then processed for both standard histology as well as immunocytochemical staining for S100 protein and T6 (CD1) antigens. These two markers demonstrated the Langerhans' cells within the epithelium. Previous studies have suggested that S100 positive Langerhans' cells may constitute a functionally active subset of antigen presenting cells. A quantitative measure of these cells was made using a computer-linked image analyser attached to a conventional microscope and a drawing tube.

One hundred and thirty women were studied, falling into three categories; 36 had normal cytology, colposcopy and histology, 39 abnormal colposcopy with changes of HPV only on histology and 55 had colposcopic and histological evidence of CIN with HPV infection.

Within each group, each of the cofactors cited above was examined for a significant effect on the Langerhans' cell counts per mm^2.

TABLE 2. Median Langerhans' cell counts per mm^2 according to histology of epithelium

	S100	T6
Normal (n = 36)	51.4	115.9
HPVI (n = 39)	41.0	87.7
CIN/HPVI (n = 55)	12.1	28.3
	$P = 0.0014$	$P < 0.0001$

(Using Wilcoxon test for trend).

The results shown in table 2 confirm the previous findings that the Langerhans' cell counts are reduced in both HPV infection and in CIN with HPV infection.

In both normal epithelium and CIN/HPV lesions the decrease in the Langerhans' cell count was found to be significantly associated with current cigarette smoking (Tables 3 and 4). These results have been presented in greater detail elsewhere.[14]

TABLE 3. Effect of cigarette smoking on Langerhans' cell count per mm^2 in normal epithelium

S100 Regression coeff	S.E.	LR Statistic	LR ratio P value
−0.0995	0.252	23.9	<0.0001

T6 Regression coeff	S.E.	LR Statistic	LR ratio P value
−0.0734	0.018	21.1	<0.0001

Using Log-linear modelling.

TABLE 4. Effect of cigarette smoking and HPV 16 positivity on Langerhans' cell count per mm^2 in CIN/HPVI lesions

S100	Regression coeff	S.E.	LR Statistic	LR ratio P value
ncigs	−0.0717	0.0060	18.2	<0.0001
HPV 16	−0.2493	0.0967	6.6	0.01

T6	Regression coeff	S.E.	LR Statistic	LR ratio P value
ncigs	−0.0311	0.0135	5.6	<0.0001
HPV 16	−0.5609	0.0760	54.1	<0.0001

Using Log-linear modelling.

TABLE 5. Effect of HPV 16 detection on Langerhans' cell count per mm^2 in epithelium showing HPVI only

S100 Regression coeff	S.E.	LR Statistic	LR ratio P value
−0.0190	0.0050	15.8	0.0001

T6 Regression coeff	S.E.	LR Statistic	LR ratio P value
−0.2050	0.0738	7.70	0.006

An association was found between the detection of HPV type 16 DNA and a decrease in the Langerhans' cell count per mm^2 in epithelium showing changes of CIN with HPV infection. Furthermore, in cervical epithelium showing evidence of HPV infection alone, HPV type 16 was found to be associated with a significant decrease in the Langerhans' cell count, as assessed by both S100 and T6 markers (Table 5). A more detailed presentation of these results can be found elsewhere.[15]

There was not significant effect of oral contraceptive use, semen exposure, or cervical infection on the Langerhans' cell counts.

DISCUSSION

The recent results support the previous findings that Langerhans' cells in cervical epithelium are diminished in both HPV infection and CIN with HPV. This may represent a progressive reduction in the integrity of the local epithelial immunity with increasing histological abnormality. In conjunction with the previously described changes in T cell numbers, this suggests that localised immunodeficiency may play an important role in the development of cervical neoplasia.

The finding[14] that cigarette smoking is associated with a reduction in the Langerhans' cell count in both normal and premalignant cervical epithelium represents the first possible mechanism to explain the epidemiological association of smoking with cervical cancer. This suggests that a local decrease in the antigen presenting capacity of the epithelium might facilitate persistent HPV infection. This would increase the likelihood of HPV DNA integration into the host cell genome, which is associated with neoplastic transformation.[16] The observed differential effect of HPV type 16 infection on Langerhans' cells also begins to explain the particular association of this viral subtype with cervical neoplasia. Further work to determine the effects of other viral subtypes on this and other facets of local immunity are currently being performed.

Cigarette smoking has previously been shown to cause several effects on host immunology: these include changes in T cell function,[17] macrophages,[18] and natural killer cells.[19] Furthermore, the finding that certain constituents of cigarette smoke are concentrated in cervical mucus[20] supports the possibility of a selective local effect on cervical immunity. However, the exact functional significance of changes in the distribution of individual cell groups awaits the development of kinetic models of cell function and the identification of the particular interactions between cells bearing different antigenic markers.

In summary, the study of changes in Langerhans' cells and other immunologically important cells within cervical epithelium may begin to explain why all women with genital HPV infection do not inevitably develop CIN and invasive cancer. Moreover, it may explain the mechanisms of action of co-factors found to be important from epidemiological studies. Certainly, the evidence that cigarette smoking may exert an immunosuppressive effect on cervical epithelium, should reinforce the need to encourage women, especially those with genital warts or abnormal smears, to stop smoking cigarettes.

REFERENCES

1 Zur Hausen H. Human genital cancer: synergism between two virus infections or synergism between a virus infection and initiating events? *Lancet* 1982;**ii**: 1370–2.
2 Pfister H. Relationship of Papillomaviruses to anogenital cancer. *Obstetrics and Gynecology Clinics of North America* 1987;**14**(2):349–61.
3 Campion M J, McCance D J, Cuzick J, Singer A. Progressive potential of mild cervical atypia: prospective cytological, colposcopic, and virological study. *Lancet* 1986;**ii**:237–40.
4 McCance D J, Campion M J, Clarkson P K, Chester P M, Jenkins D, Singer A. Prevalence of human papillomavirus type 16 DNA sequence in cervical intraepithelial neoplasia and invasive carcinoma of the cervix. *Br J Obstet Gynaecol* 1985;**92**:1101–5.
5 Meanwell C A, Blackledge G, Cox M F, Maitland N J. HPV 16 DNA in normal and malignant cervical epithelium; implications for the aetiology and behaviour of cervical neoplasia. *Lancet* 1987; **i**:703–7.
6 Editorial. Human papillomaviruses and cervical cancer: a fresh look at the evidence. *Lancet* 1987;**i**:725–6.
7 Hollingworth A, Barton S E, Jenkins D, Cuzick J, Singer A. Colposcopy of women with cervical HPV type 16 infection but normal cytology. Lancet 1987;**ii**:1148.
8 Sillman F, Stanek A, Sedlis A, Rosenthal J, Lanks, K W, Buchhagen D, Nicastri A, Boyce J. The relationship between human papillomavirus and lower genital tract intraepithelial neoplasia in immunosuppressed women. *Am J Obstet Gynecol* 1984;**150**:300–8.
9 Schneider V, Kay S, Lee H M. Immunosuppression as a high risk factor in the development of condyloma acuminatum and squamous neoplasia of the cervix. *Acta Cytologica* 1983;**27**:220–4.
10 Tay S K, Jenkins D, Maddox P, Campion M, Singer A. Subpopulations of Langerhans' cells in cervical neoplasia. *Br J Obstet Gynaecol* 1987;**94**:10–5.
11 Tay S K, Jenkins D, Maddox P, Singer A. Lymphocyte phenotypes in cervical intraepithelial neoplasia and human papillomavirus infection. *Br J Obstet Gynaecol* 1987;**94**:16–21.

12 Tay S K, Jenkins D, Maddox P, Hogg N, Singer A. Tissue macrophage response in human papillomavirus infection and cervical intraepithelial neoplasia. *Br J Obstet Gynaecol* 1987;**94**:1094–7.
13 Tay S K, Jenkins D, Singer A. Natural Killer cells in cervical intraepithelial neoplasia and human papillomavirus infection. *Br J Obstet Gynaecol* 1987;**94**: 901–6.
14 Barton S E, Maddox P H, Edwards R, Cuzick J, Jenkins D, Singer A. Effect of cigarette smoking on cervical epithelial immunity: A mechanism for neoplastic change? *Lancet* 1988;**ii**:652–4.
15 Barton S E, Hollingworth A, Maddox P H, Edwards R, Cuzick J, Jenkins D, McCance D J, Singer A. An immunopathological study of possible cofactors in the aetiology of Cervical Intraepithelial Neoplasia. *J Reprod Med* 1989 (in press).
16 Singer A, McCance D J. The wart virus and genital neoplasia; a casual or causal association. *Br J Obstet Gynaecol* 1986;**92**:1083–5.
17 Miller L G, Goldstein G, Murphy M, Ginns L C. Reversible alterations in Immunoregulatory T cells in smoking. *Chest* 1982;**5**:527–9.
18 Rasp F L, Clawson C C, Hoidal R, Repine J E. Reversible impairment of the adherence of alveolar macrophages from cigarette smokers. *Am Rev Resp Dis* 1978;**118**:979–86.
19 Fearson M, Edwards A, Lind A, Milton G W, Hersey P. Low Natural Killer cell activities and Immunoglobulin levels associated with smoking in human subjects. *Int J Cancer* 1979;**23**:603–9.
20 Sasson I, Haley N J, Hoffman D, Wynder E L, Hellberg D, Nilsson S. Cigarette smoking and neoplasia of the uterine cervix. Smoke constituents in cervical mucus. *N Engl J Med* 1985;**312**:315–6.

29

IMMUNOSUPPRESSION BY SEMINAL PLASMA: A COFACTOR IN THE AETIOLOGY OF CERVICAL NEOPLASIA?

Michael Turner

Assistant Master

National Maternity Hospital, Dublin

INTRODUCTION

Previous epidemiological studies have shown that there may be a male influence in the development of cervical neoplasia. Women have, for example, a three-fold increased risk of cervical cancer if they marry a man whose previous wife had cervical cancer.[1] A woman's risk of cervical cancer is related to her husband's occupation and is increased if his work involves travel and absence from the home.[2,3] The male partners of women with cervical neoplasia are more likely to have a history of early sexual experience, multiple sexual partners and sexually transmitted disease.[4,5,6]

A number of viruses, particularly the papillomaviruses (HPV), have been implicated in the causation of cervical neoplasia[7,8,9,10] and it has been suggested, therefore, that the male may be important in the sexual transmission of an infectious carcinogen. In a study of women who had been the sexual consorts for at least one year of men with penile condylomata acuminata, 8 out of 25 had cervical intraepithelial neoplasia.[11] In 19 out of 26 women with genital tract HPV infection, their male partner harboured the same HPV type.[12] In a study of 34 women with cervical condylomata or intraepithelial neoplasia, external evidence of HPV infection was detected in 53% (n = 18) of the male consorts.[13]

HPV infection alone, however, cannot fully explain the development of cervical neoplasia[14,15,16] and this has stimulated research into other possible aetiological factors.[17]

Seminal plasma immunosuppression

Human seminal plasma (HSP) constitutes approximately 90% of the normal volume of the ejaculate and has been shown to alter the functions of various components of the immune system including lymphocytes and natural killer cells.[18,19] It has been suggested that the physiological functions of seminal plasma immunosuppression are to prevent auto-immunisation in the male by sperm antigens, and to facilitate fertilisation of the female by inhibiting immunological destruction of spermatozoa as they pass through the lower female genital tract.[18]

The human uterine cervix normally produces a leucocytosis in response to spermatozoa,[20] but seminal plasma protects the spermatozoa possibly by abrogating the postcoital T lymphocyte response to spermatozoal histocompatibility antigens.[21] T-lymphocytes are also important in the normal host response to neoplastic and virus-infected cells[22] and T lymphocytes are concentrated around the basement membrane in cervical epithelium.[23] Inhibition of lymphocyte function, therefore, may predispose to the development of cervical neoplasia.

Epstein-Barr virus (EBV), a DNA virus like HPV, has been shown to replicate in the uterine cervix *in vivo*.[24] We used an established lymphocyte regression assay[25] to examine the effects of human seminal plasma on the normal lymphocyte response to infection with EBV.[16] The basis of this assay is the initial proliferation of foci of B lymphocytes infected with EBV and the subsequent regression of the foci due to the activity of cytotoxic memory T lymphocytes in EBV-seropositive donors.[26,27] If the donor is EBV-seronegative or if T lymphocyte function is inhibited, the foci do not regress but continue to proliferate and can be subcultured.

Seminal plasma was obtained from healthy males whose partners were attending the hospital's infertility clinic. Repeated seminal analyses were normal and a female factor was responsible for the infertility. The seminal plasma was centrifuged to remove spermatozoa and cellular debris, and dialysed twice against one litre of phosphate buffered saline to remove small molecules. It was freeze-dried at $-70°C$, and reconstituted for the experiments at a concentration of 0.5 mg per ml. Lymphocytes were isolated from EBV-seropositive donors by centrifugation through Ficoll-Hypaque, and infected with EBV.[25] These infected lymphocytes were cultured in supplemented RPMI and observed regularly in microtest wells over 4 weeks. The controls used were the culture medium alone, bovine serum albumin (BSA) as a protein control and cyclosporine (CS), which inhibits T lymphocytes, as a positive control for immunosuppression.[16]

As expected, in the normal and BSA culture wells the foci regressed and in the CS wells the foci persisted.[16] In the seminal plasma wells, the foci persisted and could be easily and repeatedly subcultured.[16] The presence of EBV in the subcultured lymphocytes was confirmed by DNA-DNA hybridisation. Immunohistochemical staining confirmed that the proliferating foci were polyclonal B lymphocytes which were positive for Epstein-Barr Nuclear Antigen (EBNA). These observations were confirmed over five separate experiments and with seminal plasma from six subjects.[16] Trypan blue exclusion studies indicated that seminal plasma in the absence of EBV had neither a direct cytotoxic nor a proliferative effect on the lymphocytes. These results indicate that human seminal plasma inhibits the normal lymphocyte response *in vitro* to infection with the Epstein-Barr virus. This effect of seminal plasma may possibly be a factor not only in the sexual transmission, persistence and reactivation of EBV, but also may have similar effects following infection with other sexually transmissable viruses,[28] including HPV.

These observations are consistent with the results obtained from other studies of the effects of human seminal plasma on lymphocyte function. HSP inhibits the generation of cytotoxic T lymphocytes in mixed lymphocyte

31

cultures.[29] In a study using pooled human seminal plasma, whole HSP and its high molecular weight fractions possessed an inhibitory effect both on lymphocytic blastogenic response to phytohaemagglutinin (PHA) and on a two-way mixed lymphocyte reaction,[30] HSP has also been shown to inhibit T-cell associated E-rosette formation.[31] *In vitro* studies of lymphocyte activation by mitogens have demonstrated that seminal plasma inhibits T cells without affecting B cells and that this inhibition could be reversed by the addition of fresh lymphocytes.[32] Many of these *in vitro* effects of seminal plasma occur with concentrations as low as 0.05% by volume.

High concentrations of seminal plasma have been reported to be cytotoxic to lymphocytes.[33] This effect is enhanced by the presence in supplemented culture medium of fetal calf serum, which contains polyamine oxidase. This enzyme oxidizes spermine and spermidine in seminal plasma to produce cytotoxic aldehydes.[19] A direct cytotoxic effect is unlikely to explain the observation in the EBV regression assay, however, because the seminal plasma concentration was low, the 2% fetal calf serum supplementation was low and the use of dialysed HSP should exclude small molecules such as spermine and spermidine. This is further supported by the absence of a direct lymphotoxic effect of the dialysed seminal plasma in the Trypan Blue exclusion studies,[16] as well as, the evidence from other studies.[33,34] Experiments to date suggest that inhibition of lymphocyte function by HSP is attributable to a large molecular weight component,[33,35] which is likely to be present in HSP which has been dialysed.

Supportive evidence

The possibility that the inhibition of lymphocyte function by seminal plasma may be a factor in the genesis of cervical neoplasia is supported by other evidence. While both cancer[36] and viral infection[37] can suppress immunity, there is evidence that prior suppression predisposes to both viral infection and neoplasia.[38] In particular, women who are systemically immunosuppressed are more likely to develop genital tract neoplasia.[39,40]

In patients with invasive cervical cancer, numerous studies have demonstrated depletion of circulating T lymphocytes.[41,42,43] In 20 patients with multicentric genital neoplasia-papilloma syndrome, subclinical immunodeficiency has been reported.[44] Compared with healthy controls, the study group had a higher proportion of T8 or suppressor lymphocytes, a lower proportion of T4 or cytotoxic lymphocytes and a lower mean T4-T8 ratio in peripheral blood. In patients with cervical intraepithelial neoplasia (CIN), an abnormal T4:T8 lymphocyte ratio in the cervical epithelium has been reported.[23] In a study of T lymphocyte ratios in the peripheral blood of 16 patients with CIN, 9 of the patients had less than 40% T4 lymphocytes.[45] The T4:T8 ratio was abnormally inverted in 7 (44%) of the patients with a mean of 1.18 (range 0.45–2.47). A possible mechanism for the action of seminal plasma on lymphocyte function is an effect on T4 or T8 lymphocytes.

Human natural killer (NK) cells are also important in the normal immune response to tumour and virus-infected cells[46] and reduced intraepithelial NK

32

cells have been reported in both CIN and HPV infection.[47] Seminal plasma has been shown to suppress NK cell activity[48,49] and NK cells have a suppressive effect on EBV-induced immunoglobulin synthesis.[50] Thus, inhibition of NK cell activity by repeated exposure to seminal plasma may also promote both viral infection and neoplasia of the cervix.[51]

Clinical implications

Should the male partner of women with cervical neoplasia be screened for HPV infection? Cytological screening for HPV is of little use in the male,[52] and the diagnosis of genital warts is best made by clinical examination in association with colposcopic examination of the penis.[13] While clinically evident HPV infection in the male should be treated, no treatment modality has been shown to eradicate completely HPV from either male or female genital tract.[53] Furthermore, there is no evidence that treatment of the male for HPV infection will reduce the subsequent incidence of neoplasia in either partner. Cervical premalignancy has been treated successfully for many years without taking the male partners into consideration. The most likely benefit of diagnosing asymptomatic HPV infection may be that the male could be warned of the risks of transmitting the virus to uninfected sexual partners. In addition, it may not be the present male partner who warrants investigation. If the cervical neoplasia has been treated adequately and a proper follow-up programme initiated, there may be nothing to be gained by overzealous pursuit of the papillomavirus in the male. Indeed, such an emphasis may compound the woman's initial gynaecological problem with subsequent sexual dysfunction and marital disharmony.[54] These iatrogenic complications may not respond as easily to therapy as the cervical neoplasia. Before routine screening of the male partner can be advocated, it must be shown to be both feasible and beneficial.

There is considerable uncertainty about the relationship between cervical neoplasia and the different methods of contraception. This is due to the virtual impossibility in any epidemiological study of controlling for all the confounding variables, for example, accurately determining the sexual histories of the study and control cases. The available studies suggest that patients taking oral contraceptives have an increased incidence of both preinvasive and invasive cervical neoplasia,[55,56,57] and that patients using barrier methods have a lower incidence.[58,59] A unifying explanation, however, for the epidemiological associations between cervical neoplasia and the different methods of contraception may be the degree of exposure of the cervix to the immunosuppressive effects of seminal plasma.

The possibility that barrier methods may have a role in the prevention and treatment of cervical neoplasia is supported by a study[60] in which 157 patients had cervical intraepithelial neoplasia (CIN) diagnosed (88 with CIN 1 or 2, 69 with CIN 3). They were treated solely by the diagnostic biopsy and advised subsequently to use a condom throughout sexual intercourse. Of the 139 patients followed up, 136 (98%) 'showed complete colposcopic and cytological reversal of the disease after an average interval of 5 months. Eight of the 11 patients who had late recurrences after 6–87 months (mean 38 months) showed complete reversal after resumption of condom use. No patient in the study showed progression of disease while relying on condoms.

The association between cervical neoplasia and sexual intercourse is inescapable and, therefore, the male must be a factor in the pathogenesis of cervical neoplasia. Specifically, the role of the male may be the transmission of an infectious carcinogen, or the suppression by seminal plasma of the woman's immune response, or both. The relative contribution of each factor is difficult to determine. To complicate matters further, the male responsible for precipitating neoplasia by suppressing cervical immunity may not be the male responsible for transmitting the original carcinogen.

Few women who are sexually active develop cervical cancer and it is important to emphasise that the immunosuppressant effects of seminal plasma are physiological and necessary for fertilisation. In the absence of a carcinogen, these effects of seminal plasma on the cervix are not harmful. Only in the presence of a carcinogen could these effects of seminal plasma be important as cofactors in the development of neoplasia. In such women it is reassuring that the cervical neoplasia can be detected early using current screening methods and effective treatment implemented.

Many questions about the male role in cervical neoplasia remain unanswered. The recent evidence that human seminal plasma inhibits the normal lymphocyte response to a viral infection is of interest because it provides an explanatory link for the virology, immunology and epidemiology of cervical neoplasia.

REFERENCES

1 Kessler II. Etiological concepts in cervical carcinogenesis. *Gynecol Oncol* 1981;**12**: S7–S24.
2 Beral V. Cancer of the cervix: a sexually transmitted disease? *Lancet* 1974;**i**: 1037–40.
3 Brown S, Vessey M, Harris R. Social class, sexual habits and cancer of the cervix. *Commun Med* 1984;**6**:281–6.
4 Buckley J D, Harris R W C, Doll R, Vessey M P, Williams P T. Case-control studies of the husbands of women with dysplasia or carcinoma of the cervix uteri. *Lancet* 1981;**ii**:1010–4.
5 Skegg D C G, Corwin P A, Paul C. Importance of the male factor in cancer of the cervix. *Lancet* 1982;**ii**:581–3.
6 Zunzunegui M V, King M C, Coria C F, Charlet J. Male influences on cervical cancer risks. *Am J Epidemiol* 1986;**123**:302–7.
7 Rapp F, Jenkins F J. Genital cancer and viruses. *Gynecol Oncol* 1981;**12**:S25–S41.
8 Zur Hausen H, De Villiers E M, Gissmann L. Papillomavirus infections and human genital cancer. *Gynecol Oncol* 1981;**12**:S124–S128.
9 Baird P J. The role of human papilloma and other viruses. *Clin Obstet Gynaecol* 1985;**12**:19–32.
10 Kaufman R H, Adam E. Herpes simplex virus and human papillomavirus in the development of cervical carcinoma. *Clin Obstet Gynecol* 1986;**29**:678–92.

11 Campion M J, Singer A, Clarkson P K, McCance D J. Increased risk of cervical neoplasia in consorts of men with penile condylomata acuminata. *Lancet* 1985; **i**:943–6.

12 Schneider A, Sawada E, Gissmann L, Shah K. Human Papillomaviruses in women with a history of abnormal papanicolaou smears and in their male partners. *Obstet Gynecol* 1987;**69**:554–62.

13 Levine R U, Crum C P, Herman E, Silvers D, Ferenczy A, Richart R M. Cervical papillomavirus infection and intraepithelial neoplasia: A study of male sexual partners. *Obstet Gynecol* 1984;**64**:16–20.

14 Kirchner H. Immunobiology of human papillomavirus infection. *Prog Med Virol* 1986;**33**:1–41.

15 Editorial. Human papillomaviruses and cervical cancer: a fresh look at the evidence. *Lancet* 1987;**i**:725–6.

16 Turner M J, White J O, Soutter W P. The male factor in cervical neoplasia. *Contemp Rev Obstet Gynaecol* 1988c;**1**:35–42.

17 Reid B L. The causation of cervical cancer: A general review. *Clin Obstet Gynaecol* 1985;**12**:1–18.

18 James K, Hargreave T B. Immunosuppression by seminal plasma and its possible clinical significance. *Immunol Today* 1984;**5**:357–63.

19 Alexander N J, Anderson D J. Immunology of semen. *Fertil Steril* 1987;**47**: 192–205.

20 Pandya I J, Cohen J. The leukocytic reaction of the human uterine cervix to spermatozoa. *Fertil Steril* 1985;**43**:417–21.

21 Thomas I K, McLean J M. Seminal plasma abrogates the postcoital T cell response to spermatozoal histocompatability antigens. *Am J Reprod Immunol* 1984;**6**: 185–9.

22 Freedman R S, Bowen J, Herson J, Wharton J T, Rutledge F N. Tumour antigenicity and the immune system in gynaecological cancer: a review. *Gynecol Oncol* 1980;**9**:43–62.

23 Tay S K, Jenkins D, Maddox P, Singer A. Lymphocyte phenotypes in cervical intraepithelial neoplasia and human papillomavirus infection. *Br J Obstet Gynaecol* 1987a;**94**:16–21.

24 Sixbey J W, Lemon S M, Pagano J S. A second site for Epstein-Barr virus shedding: the uterine cervix. *Lancet* 1986;**ii**:1122–4.

25 Crawford D H, Sweny P, Edwards J M B, Janossy G, Hoffbrand A V. Long-term T-cell-mediated immunity to Epstein-Barr virus in renal-allograft recipients receiving cyclosporin A. *Lancet* 1981;**i**:10–13.

26 Moss D J, Rickinson A B, Pope J H. Long-term T-cell-mediated immunity to Epstein-Barr virus in man. 1. Complete regression of virus-induced transformation in cultures of seropositive donor leukocytes. *Int J Cancer* 1978;**22**:662–8.

27 Rickinson A B, Moss D J, Wallace L E *et al.* Long-term T-cell-mediated immunity to Epstein-Barr virus. *Cancer Res* 1981;**41**:4216–21.

28 Turner M J, White J O, Soutter W P. Seminal plasma and AIDS. *Immunol Today* 1987;**8**:258.

29 Lord E M, Sensabaugh G F, Stites D P. Immunosuppressive activity of human seminal plasma I. Inhibition of in vitro lymphocyte activation. *J Immunol* 1977; **118**:1704–11.

30 Majumdar S, Bapna B C, Mapa M K, Gupta A N, Devi P K, Subrahmanyam D. Effect of seminal plasma and its fractions on in vitro blastogenic response to mitogen. *Int J Fertil* 1982;**27**:224–8.

31 Marcus Z H, Hess E V, Herman J H, Troiano P, Freisheim J. In vitro studies in reproductive immunology—2. Demonstration of the inhibitory effect of male genital tract constituents on PHA-stimulated mitogenesis and E-rosette formation of human lymphocytes. *J Reprod Immunol* 1979;**1**:97–107.

32 Marcus Z H, Hess E V. In vitro studies in reproductive immunology, 3. Restoration of mitogenic activity of lymphocytes inhibited by seminal plasma in man. *Arch Androl* 1981;**6**:67–74.

33 Allen R D, Roberts T K. The relationship between the immunosuppressive and cytotoxic effects of seminal plasma. *Am J Reprod Immunol Microbiol* 1986;**11**: 59–64.

34 Jacobson A H, Anderson D J. Immunosuppression by seminal plasma in vitro—an artefact? *Immunol Today* 1986;**7**:357.

35 Hess E V, Marcus Z H. The inhibitors in seminal plasma. *J Lab Clin Med* 1980;**96**: 577–81.

36 Rhodes J. Effects of tumours on the immune system. In: Endocrine Problems in Cancer (eds Jung R T, Sikora K). Heinemann Medical Books, London, 1984; pp. 299–312.

37 Rouse B T, Horohov D W. Immunosuppression in viral infections. *Rev Infect Dis* 1986;**8**:850–73.

38 Editorial. Cancer in organ transplant recipients: part of an induced immune deficiency syndrome. *Br Med J* 1984;**288**:659–60.

39 Schneider V, Kay S, Lee H M. Immunosuppression as a high-risk factor in the development of condyloma acuminatum and squamous neoplasia of the cervix. *Acta Cytol* 1983;**27**:220–4.

40 Sillman F, Stanek A, Sedlis A *et al.* The relationship between human papillomavirus and lower genital intraepithelial neoplasia in immunosuppressed women. *Am J Obstet Gynecol* 1984;**150**:300–8.

41 Rand J, Jenkins D M, Bulmer R. T- and B-lymphocyte subpopulations in pre-invasive and invasive carcinoma of the cervix. *Clin Exp Immunol* 1977;**30**: 421–8.

42 Levy S, Kopersztych S, Musatti C C, Souen J S, Salvatore C A, Mendes N F. Cellular immunity in squamous cell carcinoma of the uterine cervix. *Am J Obstet Gynecol* 1978;**130**:160–4.

43 Ishiguro T, Sugitachi I, Katoh K. T and B lymphocytes in patients with squamous cell carcinoma of the uterine cervix. *Gynecol Oncol* 1980;**9**:80–5.

44 Carson L F, Twiggs L B, Fukushima M, Ostrow R S, Faras A J, Okagaki T. Human genital papilloma infections: An evaluation of immunologic competence in the genital neoplasia-papilloma syndrome. *Am J Obstet Gynecol* 1986;**155**:784–9.

45 Turner M J, Ford M R, Barrett M, White J O, Soutter W P. T lymphocytes and cervical intraepithelial neoplasia. *Ir J Med Sci* 1988a;**158**:184.

46 Santoli D, Koprowski H. Mechanisms of activation of human natural killer cells against tumour and virus-infected cells. *Immunol Rev* 1979;**44**:125–63.

47 Tay S K, Jenkins D, Singer A. Natural killer cells in cervical intraepithelial neoplasia and human papillomavirus infection. *Br J Obstet Gynaecol* 1987b;**94**: 901–6.

48 James K, Szymaniec S. Human seminal plasma is a potent inhibitor of natural killer cell activity in vitro. *J Reprod Immunol* 1985;**8**:61–70.

49 Tarter T H, Cunningham-Rundles S, Koide S S. Suppression of natural killer cell activity by human seminal plasma in vitro: identification of 19-OH-PGE as the suppressor factor. *J Immunol* 1986;**136**:2862–7.

50 Kuwano K, Arai S, Munakata T, Tomita Y, Yoshitake Y, Kumagai K. Suppressive effect of human natural killer cells on Epstein-Barr virus-induced immunoglobulin synthesis. *J Immunol* 1986;**137**:1462–7.

51 Turner M J, White J O, Soutter W P. Natural killer cells in cervical intraepithelial neoplasia and human papillomavirus infection. *Br J Obstet Gynaecol* 1988b;**95**: 423.

52 Nahhas W A, Marshall M L, Ponziani J, Jagielo J A. Evaluation of urinary cytology of male sexual partners of women with cervical intraepithelial neoplasia and human papilloma virus infection. *Gynecol Oncol* 1986;**24**:279–85.

53 Murdoch J B, Cordiner J W, MacNab J C M. Relevance of HPV-16 to laser therapy for cervical lesions. *Lancet* 1987;**i**:1433.

54 Campion M J, Brown J R, McCance D J *et al.* Psychosexual trauma of an abnormal cervical smear. *Br J Obstet Gynaecol* 1986;**95**:175–9.

55 Piper J M. Review: Oral contraceptives and cervical cancer. *Gynecol Oncol* 1985;**22**: 1–14.

56 Brinton L A, Huggins G R, Lehman H F, Mallin K, Savitz D A, Trapido E, Rosenthal J, Hoover R. Long-term use of oral contraceptives and risk of invasive cervical cancer. *Int J Cancer* 1986;**38**:339–44.

57 Ebeling K, Nischan P, Schindler C. Use of oral contraceptives and risk of invasive cervical cancer in previously screened women. *Int J Cancer* 1987;**39**:427–30.

58 Wright N H, Vessey M P, Kenward B, McPherson K, Doll R. Neoplasia and dysplasia of the cervix uteri and contraception: a possible protective effect of the diaphragm. *Br J Cancer* 1978;**38**:273–9.

59 Melamed M R, Koss L G, Flehinger B J, Kelisky R P, Dubrow H. Prevalence rates of uterine cervical carcinoma in situ for women using the diaphragm or contraceptive oral steroids. *Br Med J* 1969;**3**:195–200.

60 Richardson A C, Lyon A B. The effect of condom use on squamous cell cervical intraepithelial neoplasia. *Am J Obstet Gynecol* 1981;**140**:909–13.

61 De-The G. Multistep carcinogenesis, Epstein-Barr Virus and human malignancies. In: Viruses in naturally occurring cancers. Cold Spring Harbor Conferences on Cell Proliferation (eds Essex M, Todaro G, zur Hausen H), 1980; p. 11–22.

DISCUSSION

Audience   Does the term 'sexually active' mean a lot of sex with one partner, sex with a lot of partners, or a lot of sex with a lot of partners?

Dr Turner   All of these definitions.

Audience   Is there not some epidemiological importance in discriminating between these meanings?

Dr Turner   The number of sexual partners is certainly important when considering the transmission of an infectious carcinogen. The frequency of sexual intercourse may be more important in terms of the immunosuppressant effects of seminal plasma.

Dr Crawford   It could of course be that the degree of immunosuppression varies between different males, so the probability of meeting a highly immunosuppressive male increases with the number of alternative partners.

Dr Turner   It may well be 'dose dependent', but it is unlikely that the amount of immunosuppressant would vary greatly from male to male. Every male is likely to have these factors in large amount.

Audience   It has been pointed out that there is no effective treatment for a male partner, so why find him, when in fact all you may be creating is marital disharmony? Multiple sexually transmitted diseases are common and there is a strong association between HPV infection and asymptomatic gonorrhoea. Is it not better to screen for the other conditions, which are amenable to treatment? Finally, has HPV been found in semen?

Dr Turner   It is necessary to distinguish between patients who have symptomatic and asymptomatic HPV infection. Yes, it is right to raise a doubt about the clinical value of screening the male patient, where the male is asymptomatic. I agree with your point about the association between other genito-urinary infections. In a collaborative study with St Mary's and the Hammersmith Hospital, we found that 40% of patients with CIN had other genito-urinary infections.

Dr McCance   To answer the second part of your question about HPV and seminal fluid, there has been one report where HPV was found in the semen of a man who was immunosuppressed. It was probably cell associated, that is, in the squamous epithelial cells sloughed off during ejaculation.

Dr Turner   There are animal studies which have shown that the papilloma virus, the herpes virus and the cytomegalovirus have been found in mice with cervical cancer. It may be that more than one virus has the potential to cause cervical cancer given sufficient local or systemic immunosuppression.

Audience   In women with CIN should one recommend the use of condoms routinely?

Dr Turner   This is an interesting point. There is a study from Richardson in the United States in which a group of 137 patients with biopsy-proven CIN were advised to use condoms. He reported a 98% regression rate of CIN in these patients, which compares favourably with other forms of treatment. He also noted that no case of CIN progressed while using the condoms, which again is evidence to suggest that exposure to the immunosuppressant effects of seminal plasma may alter the natural history of CIN.

Audience   Dr Turner, what is the immunosuppressive component of seminal plasma?

Dr Turner   I think there are a large number of immunosuppressive components. The response observed using dialysed human seminal plasma would suggest that the component responsible for inhibiting lymphocyte function is a high molecular weight protein. The possibility of some of the placental proteins being responsible has been suggested, and these have been detected, particularly the PAPP14, but the specific factor has yet to be elucidated and further work is needed.

Audience   Is there any evidence that the local immune responses in the cervix change and improve after treatment of the CIN? The HPV and the co-factors are still there after treatment and yet frequently the CIN does not recur.

Mr Barton   Dr McClean in New Zealand has studied post-laser ablation biopsies and found that Langerhans cells are present in healing epithelium. When the mature epithelium forms, it does resemble healthy epithelium, even if on a separate part of the cervix HPV DNA can be detected. This suggests that you can have recovery irrespective of the presence of HPV. Whether that is because of a direct effect on the tissue regeneration and local tissue factors allowing the Langerhans cells to occur, or a change in mucus washing over the cervix, no one is certain, and that is work that has not really been explored further.

Dr McCance   95% of CIN arises from the transformation zone. With laser ablation, it either disappears completely, or on healing is very much reduced or changed physiologically. If you get rid of the target cells, it does not matter if HPV is around, although it is associated with vulval cancer and penile cancer, but the incidence of malignant conversion at these sites is low.

Audience   If the local treatment for HPV is insufficient, what is the panel's experience of systemic treatments, like interferon?

Dr Turner   We have been treating CIN effectively for years with cone biopsy without any recurrence and without eradicating HPV entirely from the genital

39

tract, so the question should not be, 'Is there any treatment available?', but, 'Does the patient need to be treated?'

Audience   Has any work been done on the longitudinal immunological changes that occur with untreated CIN?

Mr Barton   The problem is that once the cervix has been biopsied the local immunology has been affected. We did attempt a study on the effects of changing smoking habits, by looking at sequential biopsies in eight women with uncomplicated HPVI, who had been encouraged to give up smoking. Unfortunately, at the three month review six of them had increased the amount they smoked and only two had stopped. I think that the reason for this was the psychological and psycho-sexual trauma of having an abnormal smear and worrying about it. In the six who had increased, they had actually progressed to CIN with a further diminution of Langerhans cell counts. In the two who had given up smoking, both had persistent HPVI, but one with a higher Langerhans count than she had before. That is a small study and you cannot conclude much from it except that the problem of changing smoking habits is large.

Audience   You showed a slide with what I would call koilocytosis. If you are basing your method on an area, is the assessment not skewed by taking an area where the cells are enlarged and the number of Langerhans cells reduced, and therefore is your basic methodology not questionable?

Mr Barton   No, we have addressed that question. We have looked at the cross sectional area of sequential tissue sections using both different fixation methods as well as the effects of acetic acid application on the cervix, which has an osmotic effect and changes the shape and size of the cells. We have corroborative data which supports our methodology and shows that it is very important to have controls for immunological experiments. The normal patients must undergo colposcopy in the same way, with the same strength of acetic acid, and using the same procedure. Otherwise you can get the effects you have described.

Audience   Is there evidence of a familial cause to CIN?

Dr Cuzick   There is no strong evidence to suggest a family relationship with the cause of CIN.

Dr McCance   Dr Barton, do these immunosuppressed women who smoke have other sexually transmitted infections as well?

Mr Barton   All the women treated in that study were screened for other STDs and there was a high prevalence. Four women were biopsied as part of the study, who happened also to be infected with herpes simplex. They were shedding the virus asymptomatically from areas of the cervix. In two there were signs of a herpes ulcer on the biopsy, which was visible colposcopically. In one there appeared to be a completely normal cervix, but with no Langerhans cells present in the area associated with that herpes lesion. Chlamydial infected cervices were also seen with evidence of follicle formation and there appeared to be a predominance of T8 lymphocytes with very few T4 cells. It is clear then that chlamydia or HSV do have some effect on the immunology of the cervix, but whether this affects the outcome of HPV or CIN, we do not know, and we need further studies to find out. Our study was not large enough to show a change in incidence.

Audience   Can anybody here tell us what prospects there may be for a vaccine for HPV?

Dr Crawford   It is necessary to know far more about the virus and the immune systems and the way they interact before we can think about the political and social implications of a vaccine. There are several laboratory studies in progress using various vectors. One which we particularly favour is recombinant vaccine, as a way of delivering selected pieces of the HPV-16 genome, but there are enormous difficulties in showing that it works in the absence of an adequate model in animals. There will be difficulties at the political level, since something which intervenes against the initial infection, against the coat protein, would have to be administered to pre-sexually active girls. If one attempts to attack the transformed cells, although there is little evidence for anything virus coded in that state, then that might be a more possible approach. However, the transformation protein might be involved in the expression of these premalignant cells, and that would complicate the issue further, as you would be talking about administering a vaccine which actually coded for a transforming protein and that would be difficult to accept. It is a problem which many people are working on, but I think it would be very unwise to expect a practical solution in the immediate future.

IS CERVICAL CYTOLOGY STILL USEFUL IN DIAGNOSIS?

Dr Elizabeth F D Mackenzie
Consultant Cytopathologist
Southmead Hospital, Bristol

INTRODUCTION

Cervical carcinoma causes the death of 2000 women annually in England and Wales. This number is small when compared with carcinoma of the breast (13 500) or carcinoma of the lung (7800), but cervical carcinoma if diagnosed at its preinvasive stage can be cured in almost 100% of cases.

The lead time for change from normality to invasive disease is from five to thirty-five years. Instances of rapidly progressing lesions in young women are well known. Less quoted, but certainly seen in Bristol, are examples of this rapidly invasive carcinoma in all ages; fortunately this is an uncommon finding.

The idea of a screening programme is to detect preinvasive disease of the cervix and to allow early treatment. Unfortunately many women are presenting themselves for their first smear when they have signs and symptoms of the disease, with no previous history of taking part in the screening programme. Sadly, despite the considerable efforts put into the screening programme, there has been little change in the mortality from this disease in England and Wales over the past thirty years.

THE AVON SCREENING PROGRAMME

The Avon Screening Programme provides a service for three of the District Health Authorities in Avon, Bristol and Weston, Frenchay and Southmead, with a population of a quarter of a million women between the ages of 20 and 64. The Cytology Department at Southmead was set up as a designated laboratory mainly due to public and political pressure in 1966, with little thought to the future, to the monitoring that would be required, or the problems and questions that it would create. It was in the forefront of computerisation of records and this took place in 1977. In conjunction with the Family Practitioners Committee (FPC) recall started immediately, with computerised call-up starting in 1980, although initially small and based on GP practice requests. Worldwide studies on the intensity of screening do demonstrate a relationship between an efficient screening programme and a falling death rate from cervical carcinoma. British Columbia started its screening programme in 1949 and the mortality was initially 28 per 100 000, 25 years later the figure was round 4 per 100 000 women.[1] Generally, United Kingdom screening programmes have not been efficient and compared with the Scandinavian countries, very poor indeed.[2] The exception to this has been Scotland. In Aberdeen[3] and Dundee[4] they started screening early having realised the benefits of this test. The programmes were based on a stable population, were planned and the results monitored, and there is now a demonstrable fall in mortality. The controversy over the length of screening intervals continues. A comprehensive survey, the IARC Report,[5] suggested that a three-yearly interval between tests is the optimum time interval. Many authorities agree that this would be ideal but these results were obtained in screening programmes where there was comprehensive cover of the population screened, which is patently not the case in this country. Until the population is covered comprehensively with a five-yearly screening interval, the smears monitored rigorously, with refusal of those opportunistically screened who are not due for recall and whose previous smear was negative, there is no point in reducing the screening time, as this will only increase the screening of young women i.e. those least at risk of dying from the disease. To organise the screening programme properly takes time, considerable organisation and money. The results from Finland more than support the concept of a five-yearly programme as they have had a remarkable reduction in mortality and incidence of both invasive and pre-invasive disease with a screening programme which screens women from 35–55 years at five-yearly intervals.[6]

Funding is a major consideration when establishing a new service, and later when maintaining it. Despite the edict from the DHSS in 1987 which called for more comprehensive cervical screening and the document produced in January 1988 stating the requirements of the service[7] no extra monies were made available. The two other priority issues at that time, AIDS and drug abuse, were treated differently, with extra financial support from central funds.

In maintaining the service, the attitude of the medical profession as a whole needs to be addressed, and monies found in spite of the views of those sceptics who wish to minimise the proven benefits of a comprehensive screening programme for cervical cancer.

EPIDEMIOLOGICAL DIFFICULTIES

Epidemiological analysis requires patients, not smears. The DHSS statistics are based on the number of smears, not the number of individual people screened. During the period 1968–85, 44.5 million smears were taken from 16 million women. The population should have been covered at least twice, and probably three times. This has not been the case as young women are screened repeatedly. Twenty-four per cent of smears are from women under the age of 25, who have 1% of the disease and 0.5% of the deaths, whereas 35% of the smears are from women over the age of 35 who have 86% of the disease and 95% of the deaths. Conversely, with preinvasive disease of the cervix, over 50% of the women who develop CIN3 are under 35, but the majority of women dying are over the age of 35 and half are over the age of 65; this latter group the screening programme does not cover.

It is important to educate the population at risk and target that population with the appropriate propaganda coverage if comprehensive cover of these women is to be achieved. As most of the women who are in need of a screening test, i.e. those who have never had a smear, are probably in social classes 4 and 5, or are over the age of 50, it is difficult to persuade these women to come forward.

PROVISION OF CLINICS

Opportunistic screening was encouraged before computerisation, and undertaken largely at family planning, antenatal and postnatal clinics. Now that computerisation of records and results is being undertaken in the UK, this is a difficult doctrine to replace. While it is important that this primary health care procedure should remain with general practitioners, the timing and demand for screening requires replanning with more emphasis placed on the older woman who does not present herself for screening. Most of the health screening that takes place at work mainly covers the younger age range, i.e. those who are already adequately covered by the screening programme.

Colposcopy Clinics

Colposcopy clinics will be required to deal with the problems found by the screening programme. This is a question yet to be properly addressed throughout the country not only from the provision of actual clinics and the maintaining of these clinics by properly trained gynaecologists, but to decide at what stage of cytological abnormality should the patient be referred. This varies across the country and in some instances clinics are overwhelmed by women with minor degrees of change who, if monitored with repeat cytology, would not require referral.

LABORATORY STAFFING AND MORALE

In many District General Hospital laboratories routine cervical cytological screening tests constitute up to 90% of the workload. This requires trained and skilled laboratory staff for this onerous yet key role of primary screener. The image of a 'shopping basket' screener must be altered, the service depends on the recruitment of properly trained and dedicated personnel whose skill is the key to the screening service provided. Approximately 70–80% of the gynaecological smears processed in a routine laboratory will only be seen by the primary screener and it is vital that these people are of the highest calibre and properly supervised. The odium that afflicts the service when any mistake is made and reported in the media is quite out of proportion and unjust when factors such as the quality of smear, staffing and workload are not taken into account. It is hard indeed to see how the right calibre of person will be attracted to the task when the remuneration is derisory and provision of training poor.

It is only recently that the Royal College of Pathologists has considered and implemented a mandatory training programme in cytopathology for junior medical staff who will ultimately, when they are consultants, be in charge of the laboratory side of the screening programme and responsible for the quality of the service provided by their laboratories.

RECORDS

A screening service cannot possibly run efficiently unless the data is computerised, accessible and can be analysed. In fact, from the inception of the screening programme in the 1960's all the forms and relevant material were computerised and the collation of this data was available to the DHSS from day one but, regretfully, advantage was not taken of this and consequently the opportunity was lost. There has recently been a rush to accomplish the computerisation of the records in both laboratories and FPCs based on the erroneous theory that if documents are computerised, the screening programme difficulties would be thus totally rectified and the staffing requirements in the records department would be reduced. This is totally wrong, as those of us involved in computerisation realise; the number of staff required often remains the same, but they are used more efficiently. Unless there is also uniformity of objectives amongst the laboratories and FPCs, the collection of proper data is hampered. The British Society of Clinical Cytology (BSCC) has recently produced a document to aid screening managers when they are starting to undertake computerisation of their laboratories[7].

THE ABNORMAL CYTOLOGY REPORT

The correlation between minor degrees of abnormality diagnosed cytologically and the ultimate histological outcome is controversial. John Giles and the team from the Royal Free Hospital recently presented their findings which highlighted the point that it is not poor cytology but inadequate smear taking that results in poor diagnosis.[8]

An inadequate smear is one where there is:
(i)   insufficient cellular material;
(ii) the cellular material is obscured by polymorphs;
(iii) there is an absence of endocervical cells or material from the transformation zone, particularly when there is a previous history of disease or present signs and symptoms.

There has been much controversy concerning the presence of endocervical cells as the absolute criterion for an adequate sample. If so, how has it been possible to diagnose so much preinvasive disease with 'inadequate specimens'? In many laboratories up to half of the workload would need repeating if the absence of endocervical cells was the major criterion for 'a satisfactory specimen'.

Most major cervical cancer programmes have been undertaken using the Ayre's spatula, although the Aylesbury modification is probably a more appropriate instrument. However, if used properly, the Ayre's spatula is adequate and the lack of a good smear is more likely to be due to the lack of skill on the part of the taker of the smear. There are now courses organised for practice nurses by the Royal College of Nursing, although in our area we have organised our own to include a practical component. This includes the taking of smears and the assessment by the laboratory of the quality of the smear, to ensure the skill of the trainee.

NEW ALTERNATIVE TESTS

Automation

Automated screening is one answer to the problem of reading large numbers of smears. Little progress has been made over the past twenty-five years towards solving the problems of designing a machine which will look at the specimens currently being presented on slides and which can distinguish with certainty the differences between, for example, groups of polymorphs and an abnormal nucleus. Alternatively, if the types of specimen which can be read by the machines currently being assessed are to be obtained, the whole method of collecting material for the cervical screening programme would need to be changed. Because of cost and the poor results from preliminary trials of these instruments, this seems unrealistic for the foreseeable future.

Biochemical tests

In 1987, Singer and colleagues, produced a preliminary paper on the Use of the Estimations of Octadeca-9,11,-Dienoic Acid in the Diagnosis of Cervical Neoplasia.[8] This appeared initially to be a relatively simple and accurate test, and as most clinical pathology departments have the equipment, relatively cheap and simple to introduce. Unfortunately, these results have not been verified elsewhere, and a recent paper from Guildford[9] found that there was absolutely no correlation between the test result and the presence of cervical disease.

Cervicography

Cervicography has been another recent development.[10] This last requires a special camera, which does not require expertise to use, and a photograph taken of the cervix exposed at speculum examination. This is then sent away for assessment by a trained colposcopist. In the first series it certainly did show up every minor degree of abnormality, but it had an unacceptable false positive rate of some 400%. More recently in a prospective study by this same group, it has been demonstrated that it is not an appropriate screening test but may be useful in the managing of minor degrees of abnormality. Where there are colposcopy clinics with long waiting lists cervicography could be used to try and sort out those women who require more urgent referral. The time taken for this second visit, the distress to the patient, the cost and the ultimate usefulness of the technique has yet to be properly evaluated.

IN CONCLUSION

In any screening programme it is important to identify the population at risk. With computerisation, both in the laboratory and in the FPC practitioner service this may at last be possible. The call and recall service needs to be well organised and those responsible identified.

The funding of the laboratories must be adequate, this is vital yet so often forgotten. It is necessary to provide enough skilled and trained staff, and the right environment in which to work. There must be sufficient consultant pathologists with an interest in the service to deal with the management of this large volume of work which could overwhelm Histology/Cytology Departments, as it has done in the past. The disease that is found must be referred, and well organised colposcopy units are required. The results must be monitored both locally and nationally and research encouraged.

The careful collection and management of data from all aspects of the service will in the future provide opportunities to make and alter nationwide screening policy decisions, the most controversial areas being the time interval between smears and the referral of minor degrees of abnormality. The results of a properly organised and managed screening programme will lead to a reduction in mortality from carcinoma of the cervix as has been demonstrated in other national screening programmes and lives will be saved.

REFERENCES

1 Anderson G H, Boyes D A, Benedet J L *et al*. Organisation and Results of the Cervical Cytology Screening Programme in British Columbia 1955–85. *Br Med J* 1988;**296**:975–8.
2 Laara D, Day N E, Hakama M. Trends in Mortality from Cerival Cancer in the Nordic Countries: Association with Organised Screening Programmes. *Lancet* 1987;**i**:1247–9.
3 MacGregor J E, Teper S. Mortality from Carcinoma of Cervix Uteri in Britain. *Lancet* 1978;**ii**:774–6.
4 Duguid H L D, Duncan I D, Currie J. Screening for Cervical Intraepithelial Neoplasia in Dundee and Angus 1962–81 and its Relation with Invasive Cervical Cancer. *Lancet* 1985;**ii**:1053–6.
5 Iarc Working Group Report. Screening for Squamous Cervical Cancer: Duration of Low Risk after Negative Results of Cervical Cytology and its Implication for the Screening Policies. *Br Med J* 1986;659–64.
6 Hakama M. Effect of Population Screening for Carcinoma of the Uterine Cervix in Finland. *Maturitas* 1985;**7**:3–10.
7 The Requirements of a Laboratory Computer for Cervical Screening. Prepared by the Computer Working Party of the British Society for Clinical Cytology. Obtainable from Dr Amanda Herbert, Department of Pathology, Southampton General Hospital, Tremona Road, Shirley, Southampton, Hants SO9 4XY.

8 Giles J A, Derry A, Crow J, Walker P. The Predictive Value of Repeat Cytology in Women with Mildly Dyskaryotic Smears. *Br J Obs & Gynae* (in press).
9 Singer A, Tay S K, Griffen J F A, Wickens D G, Dormandy T L. Diagnosis of Cervical Neoplasia by the Estimation of Octadeca-9,11,-Dienoic Acid. *Lancet* 1987;**i**:537–9.
10 Green A J, Starkey B J, Halloran S P, McKee G, Sutton C J, Manners B T, Walker A W. Diagnostic Significance of Octadeca-9,11,-Dienoic Acid in Cervical Neoplasia. *Lancet* 1988;**ii**:309–11.
11 DHSS Health Circular HC(88)1, HC(FP)(88)2.

NEW METHODS IN DIAGNOSIS: OF ANY VALUE?

Mr A Singer

Consultant

Obstetrics & Gynaecology

Whittington Hospital, London

INTRODUCTION

The intention is to consider some of the newer methods that have been proposed; three major tests that have been in the medical news over the last year or so and two minor ones. Each will be reviewed and an attempt made to answer the pertinent question 'Are they of any value?' Finally, the question of how cervical cancer and cervical precancer ought to be detected will be discussed.

The methods in question are:
1. automated biochemical analysis,
2. cervicography and
3. viral typing.

The major screening technique is still undoubtedly cytology. It is the best method available and it is where our energies should be directed. It should, however, not stop the search for other screening methods. Approximately 4 000 000 smears are taken annually in this country, producing 7000 slides for every cytotechnician per year. That is an enormous demand both in terms of the quantity and also the quality of the people that need to be recruited to read them. It seems that this load is too much for the present system to manage efficiently.

False negative rates for cytological analysis are reputed to be between 10 and 50%. This is not only due to interpretation problems but also to collection of the specimens. The sheer volume of work mitigates against an efficient system. That has prompted many to see if cytology can be helped by using complimentary techniques i.e. the automated biochemical tests.

AUTOMATED BIOCHEMICAL TESTS

Dr Dormandy at the Whittington Hospital has looked at the extraction of fatty acids from cell membranes in the form of octadeca-9,11-dienoic acid. The isolation of these so-called free radicals may be useful in diagnosing cervical cancer and precancer, specifically octadeca-9,11-dienoic acid 18:2 (9,11) and (9,12). It is believed that (9,12) is the parent compound, and that the transformed end product is the so-called (9-11).

It was decided to study the molar ratio, the observed 9-11 over the expected 9-12. Biopsy specimens of normals and cervical precancer were first analysed and results looked highly encouraging. The initial design was to make it a

49

complimentary test to cytology. The preliminary results appeared to show that the molar ratio was elevated in cervical cancer, precancer and with human papilloma virus infection. There was a suggestion that anerobic commensals might be generating some 9–11. The preliminary data from the Whittington was published in the Lancet in March 1988. The results were exciting.[1]

The second phase studies were then commenced in mid 1988; standards were given to a number of groups who set about repeating the original study. A larger series was also started by John Fairbanks—in this department, who has colposcoped and biopsied 500 women with a history of repeat normal cytology, or mild dyskaryosis. The results were not as hoped and there was on analysis an enormous scatter between the groups with CIN and no CIN.[2] It was therefore not possible to repeat the preliminary results. It appears that at the moment this test is of limited relevance to automated screening for cytology. The cause resides in the fact that there is a multiplicity of organisms in the vagina. On this test the organism that was causing the mischief was lacto-bacillus brevus, a commensal of the vagina and of the skin. It manufactures 9-11 and it may be that this organism has been giving false results for many years.

Microdensitometry is a technique that has been studied for a long time. A team at the Middlesex are continuing with its development which involves the staining of the chromophore with Schiff's reagents and analysis with a microdensitometer.[3] It is a simple technique which has undergone modification. Good results are claimed with a high specifity, however, the costs of a field trial are high and at the moment it is not a method that will be readily automated.

CERVICOGRAPHY

The need for this development is the patient load. In this unit 42% of patients are diagnosed as having minor cytological abnormalities. These are the so-called mild dyskaryotics with recurrent inflammatory and viral smears; a collection of smears that confuse the GP and alarm. They are collectively called borderline smears. Are women with them worth treating? or should they be ignored? We and others have shown that one third of the mild dyskariotic smears originate from patients with carcinoma in situ or indeed microinvasive carcinoma.[3] They would seem to be worth screening. Recent work from this unit also suggests that aneuploidy exists within 80–90% of CIN 1 lesions. This is surprising in a mild condition especially as aneuploidy is a sign of malignancy.

After two borderline smears, women with them should be referred for colposcopy. The problem is that it is not possible to colposcope everyone. At the Whittington Hospital in North London we have 40 colposcopy appointments a week. The average referral number is in fact 60–80. The waiting time for colposcopy for women with these smears in early 1987 was between 6 and 9 months.

Cervicography has helped to reduce this waiting time. This technique was devised in the United States by Professor Stafel from Milwaukee in 1971. We have used it in order to ease this enormous problem of patient numbers. Cervical photography—as cervicography was introduced is a triage method used to determine which patients needed colposcopy.

Forty photographs a week are now being taken by the nursing staff in the clinic, after a short counselling session. It is also important to be able to reassure a woman that she does not have cancer. She may have a lesion consistent with CIN 1 or have HPV infection, and she can then be reassured. A further cervicography and smear (including an endocervical brush smear) is taken in 12 months. If the lesion is still apparent it can be destroyed by local methods. Lesions of a more serious nature corresponding to CIN 2-3 are referred to colposcopy.

For follow up after laser cone biopsy, cervicography plus brush sample is invaluable. At the Whittington Hospital in 1988, nearly 3000 women were treated with cone biopsy or laser evaporation, and it would not be possible to see this number of follow ups otherwise. If there is anything suspicious in either of these tests, the patient is brought back for follow up.

By reducing the load of women with borderline smears it is possible to examine more quickly those with serious cytological abnormalities by colposcopy and spend more time with them in counselling. No matter how minor or how serious their smear, women are emotionally disturbed by it. Last year we showed that 80% of women who had come to the clinic, who had had either colposcopy or laser treatment, had suffered some psychological reaction, mostly psychosexual.[4] These women are now being counselled before the procedure by the sister or her trained staff and then the photograph is taken.

The preliminary results for our cervicography study of women with borderline smears are encouraging. Each woman, after cervicography, was referred for colposcopy and an endocervical brush smear, and a biopsy was taken of each abnormal area. From the first 450 women colposcoped major grade lesions, CIN 1 and 2, were found in 15%. Approximately 50% were completely normal both cytologically and colposcopically. The sensitivity of this technique is 92–93%. In this study only 2 women with minor lesions i.e. CIN 1, were missed by cervicograph and brush smear. All the major lesions were picked up. Since June 1987, as a result of the introduction of cervicography, the waiting time for women with borderline smears has been reduced from 6 to 9 months, to 4 to 5 weeks. In addition the urgent smears are now seen within two weeks of referral. This technique will not replace cytology but work with it to increase the accuracy and efficiency of managing cervical neoplasia.

HUMAN PAPILLOMA VIRUS TYPING

Many American Journals display glowing advertisements for commercial tests for detection human papillome virus (HPV) 11, 16 and 18. Are our Americans colleagues correct in suggesting viral typing as a diagnostic technique? HPV 16 and 18 have been isolated in the precancerous cervix and the vulva, in perianal disease, and in invasive cancer.

Is this method of value? A study by Campion from this unit recorded the progress of 100 women with mild cervical atypia, followed every 3 months with cytology, viral typing and colpophotography.[5] Twenty-six of these 100 progressed to CIN 3 cytologically and on colpophotography. They were not biopsied because the moment a biopsy is taken the whole immunological and biological milieu is altered. HPV 16 was found in 22 of the 26 that progressed but in only 9 of 74 that remained.

It would appear then that a woman with HPV 16 infection had a higher risk of progression to these lesions. The problem is that there is a significant prevalence of HPV 16 in CIN 1, 2 and 3, and also in other cancers or pre-cancers of the tract. It is seen in ordinary vaginal warts and it is hard to believe that even if all overt warts are removed that the viruses i.e. HPV, in sub-clinical lesions, will disappear. Recent studies have shown that HPV 16 is found to occur in 70–80% of normal sexually active women. A large prospective study is at present underway in this unit of women with negative cytology but with HPV 16 who are being followed colposcopically and cytologically.

The problem does not stop here, 60% of males whose partners have CIN 3 will have HPV infections and many HPV 16.[6] This has also been reported by a French and North American group. HPV would appear to be universal in both males and females. It may also be found around the anus and in the anal canal from which it may be shedding and causing contamination. Therefore any HPV 16 found may not necessarily originate from the genital tract but from the lower bowel. With such information it is difficult to recommend HPV typing. At the moment there seems little justification in buying these typing kits.

SUMMARY

The way to diagnose cervical cancer is by being alert to the symptoms and the signs. Cytology is not much help with gross invasive cancer, the smear is usually unsatisfactory. On the other hand precancer of the cervix (CIN 1-2 and microinvasion) does need a test and at the moment the only one of proven value is cytology, with cervicography, of value in the evaluation of women with borderline cytology. Of the remainder some are no longer valid while others are still under investigation.

REFERENCES

1 Singer A, Griffin J F A, Tay S K, Wickens D G, Dormandy T L. Diagnosis of cervical neoplasia by the estimation of octadeca-9,11-dienoic acid. *Lancet* 1987;**i**:537–9.
2 Fairbank J, Ridgway L, Griffin J, Wickens D, Singer H, Dormandy T L. Octadeca-9,11-dienoic acid in diagnosis of cervical intraepithelial neoplasia. *Lancet* 1988; **ii**:329.
3 Tay S K, Jenkins D, Singer A. Management of squamous atypia (borderline nuclear abnormalities); repeat cytology or colposcopy? *Aust N Z J Obstet Gynaecol* 1987; **27**: 140–1.

4 Campion M J, Brown J R, McCance D J *et al.* Psychosexual trauma of an abnormal cervical smear. *Br J Obstet Gynaecol* 1988; **95**:175–81.
5 Campion M J, Cuzick J, McCance D J, Singer A. Progressive potential of mild cervical atypia: prospective cytological, colposcopic, and virological study. *Lancet* 1986; **ii**:237–40.
6 Campion M J, McCance D J, Mitchell H S, Jenkins D, Singer A, Oriel J D. Subclinical penile human papillomavirus infection and dysplasia in consorts of women with cervical neoplasia. *Genitourin Med* 1988;**64**:90–9.

DISCUSSION

Audience   You said that cervicography plus endocervical brush was a good screen for minor smear abnormality. Would an Aylesbury smear with an endocervical brush do as well?

Mr Singer   I am not sure the comparison has been done between the Aylesbury and the endocervical brush. Sometimes the endocervix is so small, certainly after it has been treated, and by laser or diathermy and it is impossible to get the wooden Aylesbury spatula into the endocervix. The brush goes a lot higher. We are also now picking up endocervical abnormal gladular lesions. It is certainly of value with these. I believe that the Aylesbury is a great improvement on the Ayres spatula but I do not think it is as sensitive as the endocervical brush.

THE PLACE OF COLPOSCOPY

Dr M C Anderson

Senior Lecturer in Pathology

The Samaritan Hospital, London

INTRODUCTION

The aim of this discussion is to consider the changing place of colposcopy from 1973 to 1988. 1973 was the year that the colposcopy clinic opened at the Samaritan Hospital.

Colposcopy had been around for nearly 50 years by then, but over these 15 years the procedure has continued to change, and attitudes have become modified by events.

1973

Colposcopy was used to determine the extent of the lesion. The limits of the lesion were identified and sites selected for biopsy in the belief that colposcopy would allow the most abnormal area to be biopsied. It is important for purposes of quality control in cytology, to tell the cytologist the histological diagnosis of the lesion on which he has already made a cytological prediction. It was further hoped that invasive carcinoma could be excluded. Treatment was tailored both to the lesion and to the patient.

In 1973 little use was made of local ablation therapy. A few centres were using cryosurgery, some people were using deep diathermy, but most were not indulging in local destructive treatment. The majority of patients were being treated by cone biopsy, so colposcopy was used really to see which patients would need only a shallow cone biopsy to remove the lesion adequately. The colposcopic assessment of invasive disease on the cervix was not all that important because if a little early invasion was missed it did not matter; it was going to be removed and identified by the cone biopsy. Women were being seen during pregnancy; it was hoped that invasion could be excluded by colposcopy, so that no interference need take place before the birth.

Concepts were simple: Acetowhite epithelium, by and large, was CIN, or so it was thought, and the patients were having a tailored cone biopsy in the operating theatre to treat them.

1975 onwards—The recognition of HPV[1]

The increasing recognition of HPV has clouded the apparent precision of colposcopic diagnosis. Colposcopic lesions were now either CIN or HPV, or a combination of the two. In addition, the presence of HPV and the knowledge that was being accrued about HPV made clinicians more aware of the multi-focal nature of the disease, and of the need for vaginal and vulval examination.

Herpes Simplex Virus, by contrast, did not make much difference to the use of colposcopy. It was only rarely identified.

1978—Local destructive techniques

From 1978 onwards there was a dramatic increase in the use of local destructive methods with the introduction of the laser. The Samaritan Hospital started using it towards the end of 1978 but 2 or 3 other departments in the United Kingdom had already been using it for a year or so by that time. Soon afterwards came the SEMM caloric coagulator. As a result, the amount of local destructive treatment performed increased enormously.[2] It now became obligatory to exclude invasive carcinoma by colposcopic examination and it was important that the canal was adequately assessed. In the United Kingdom it was not felt necessary to recommend endocervical curettage as part of the work-up of a patient for local destructive treatment. This was different from the teaching in the United States, where a negative endocervical curettage was, and still is, considered mandatory for any patient having local destructive treatment. The feeling here was that if there was any doubt at all about what was happening in the canal, then the patient should have had a diagnostic and therapeutic cone biopsy. Assessing the canal is something which is much more difficult than many people appreciate and it is something which it is vital to get right if local destructive methods of treatment are to be used.

The need to be absolutely certain of diagnosis at colposcopy, due to the increase in local ablation, was probably the single most important modifying influence over the 15 years, and has altered greatly the attitude to the use of the colposcope.

1983—Adenocarcinoma *in situ*

Adenocarcinoma *in situ* was described as long ago as 1953.[3] The less severe glandular abnormalities are termed the glandular atypias, and may be mild or severe. Both became widely recognised about 1983, and diagnosed more frequently. Unfortunately colposcopy is rarely helpful in the diagnosis, and one must question the view that endocervical curettage is not a useful procedure. It may pick up glandular lesions that cannot be recognised colposcopically.

Histologically adenocarcinoma *in situ* presents with budding of the glands and a denser epithelium, due to a higher nucleocytoplasmic ratio.[4] The architecture is disturbed, but not grossly. The lesion should be recognised cytologically, but there are problems. One is that endocervical adenocarcinoma *in situ* may not affect the surface epithelium. Examples are described in which only the crypts are involved. Accordingly, cytology might not detect exfoliated cells from this.

A second problem is that histologists are not agreed on the distinction between adenocarcinoma *in situ*, and invasive adenocarcinoma. This is partly a question of the interpretation put to the proliferation (the 'tunnel clusters') around the gland crypts. Colposcopically, the lesions are defined even less well and it is very difficult, if not impossible, to recognise them.

Adenocarcinoma *in situ* is associated with squamous CIN on the cervix in 50% to 75% of cases. This can present great difficulties for the cytologic and colposcopic diagnoses. A cervical smear with a large number of squamous dyskaryotic cells may easily hide a few highly undifferentiated cells, and the diagnosis of glandular abnormality may not be made. Similarly, at colposcopy, with a cytology report of severe dyskaryosis, a squamous abnormality is expected and may cloud further observation. A biopsy may confirm the squamous abnormality and the patient is treated by local destructive methods with the clinician totally unaware of the associated adenocarcinoma *in situ*. The existence of adenocarcinoma *in situ* is therefore an important factor that must modify the place of colposcopy.

Ten years of follow-up

Local destructive methods were used from about 1978. Since 1985 a register has been kept by the British Society for Colposcopy and Cervical Pathology of the women who have developed invasive cancer after destructive treatment, most after laser therapy. Carcinomas are developing, exactly as might be expected; they developed after cone biopsy and hysterectomy. There are 26 patients in the register with squamous cell carcinomas, adenocarcinomas and adenosquamous carcinomas. Many of these patients returned with invasive carcinoma at the first follow-up 4 months after treatment. That points strongly to the fact that they were probably not accurately diagnosed at first colposcopy. They had an invasive carcinoma that was not recognised. This point is emphasised by the result of a study undertaken between 1973 to 1984.[5] The patients were seen in the colposcopy clinic at the Samaritan Hospital and in the first six years all treated by cone biopsy, as was the normal practice at that time.

During these 12 years, 33 women were found to have preclinical invasive carcinoma of the cervix of whom 27 had been examined colposcopically. In 63%, colposcopic examination was unsatisfactory, with lesions passing into the cervical canal. Nine had atypical vessels and six an irregular surface contour. However, only two had atypical vessels as the only indication for cone biopsy and 14 had canal extension as the only contraindication to local destructive treatment. This finding underlines the importance of recognising when canal involvement is present, as this feature was found in more patients with microinvasion than were atypical vessels. Three patients from the first six year period had no colposcopic features of invasion and transformation zones that did not pass into the canal; they would have been deemed suitable for local destructive treatment had that modality been in use at that time.

56

It is certain, therefore, that a number of patients with invasive carcinoma at colposcopic assessment are being treated by local destructive methods for invasive carcinoma and probably also for glandular abnormalities.

FUTURE MANAGEMENT

There are arguments for abandoning local destructive methods of treatment for CIN completely and performing excisional procedures on all patients. Accurate histological confirmation would then be possible and would exclude invasion and glandular lesions. It has been said in defence of local destructive methods of treatment, that if an experienced cytologist looks at the smear and evidence of invasion is not recognised, and if an experienced colposcopist looks at the cervix and sees no suggestion of invasion and taking a directed biopsy from the worst area that does not show invasion, the invasion, if present, is going to be so small and so insignificant that it does not matter. That statement must now be questioned.

If treatment is possible at the first visit it has an important bearing on the waiting list for colposcopy clinics. If the patient is prepared suitably, and psychologically ready, there is no reason why following colposcopy, if the lesion is suitable, treatment is not carried out in the out-patients, by an excisional procedure; a laser or loop excision with local anaesthesia. The same selection criteria for selecting patients for local destructive treatment can be employed. A lesion that goes into the canal, or one with a suspicion of invasion would not be appropriate and these patients should be referred for a formal in-patient cone biopsy, although in years to come it may be that even this line is going to get blurred.[6]

Against this argument the first and foremost problem is the histopathology workload. However, if a patient is having one visit rather than two and without diagnostic biopsies the difference narrows.

It has been said that first time excisional procedures produce more complications, but there is no evidence that this is so. The complication rate appears to be related most to the depth of procedure and the outpatients excision procedure will cause the same defect as vaporisation.

Finally, the length of the procedure is thought to be longer for laser excision as opposed to vaporisation procedures. From personal experience this is not so. It can take a very long time to vaporise a large lesion on the transformation zone but with an excisional procedure less tissue is vaporised and it takes place more quickly.

SUMMARY

In 1988 cytology, colposcopy and histology remain the mainstays in the diagnosis of CIN. Colposcopy is used to determine the extent of the lesion with directed biopsies as wished. An outpatient excision, rather than vaporisation, may follow having determined whether the lesion goes into the canal. Colposcopy is therefore good at excluding early stages of invasive carcinoma but it has its limits. It remains however a crucial step in the management of the woman with an abnormal cervical smear.

REFERENCES

1 Meisels A, Morin C, Casas-Cordero M. Human papillomavirus infection of the human uterine cervix. *Int J Gynecol Pathol* 1982;**1**:75–94.
2 Anderson M C. Treatment of cervical intraepithelial neoplasia with the carbon dioxide laser: report of 543 patients. *Obstet Gynecol* 1982;**59**:720–5.
3 Friedell G, McKay D G. Adenocarcinoma in situ of the endocervix. *Cancer* 1953;**6**: 887–97.
4 Östör A G, Pagano R, Davoren R A M, Fortune D W, Chanen W, Rome R. Adenocarcinoma *in situ* of the cervix. *Int J Gynecol Pathol* 1984;**3**:179–90.
5 Anderson M C. Are we vapourising microinvasive lesions? In: *Gynaecological laser surgery. Proceedings of the Fifteenth Study Group of the Royal College of Obstetricians and Gynaecologists*. Ithaca, USA: Perinatology Press, 1986; 127–35.
6 McIndoe A, Robson M S, Tidy J A, Mason W P, Anderson M C. Laser excision rather than vaporization: the treatment of choice for cervical intraepithelial neoplasia. *Obstet Gynecol* 1989. In press.

DISCUSSION

Mr Soutter   What would your criteria be for performing these excisions in the outpatients department? Are there some patients whom you would not include as being suitable for that kind of treatment?

Dr Anderson   The selection of patients for laser excision is exactly the same as it would be for laser oblation. In other words you colposcope the patient, and if you can see the whole of the transformation zone, and it does not go appreciably into the canal, and you can see no suggestion of invasion and no suggestion of glandular lesion you can perform an excisional procedure which will go down to 1 cm or thereabouts. If you have more canal involvement than that and you are experienced with the technique then you may perhaps do a deeper excision.

TREATMENT OF CERVICAL INTRAEPITHELIAL NEOPLASIA

Mr I D Duncan
Senior Lecturer/Honorary Consultant
Dept of Obstetrics & Gynaecology
Ninewells Hospital
Dundee

The general acceptance that cervical cytology screening programmes can and do prevent the development of invasive cancer has been followed by an increased demand for cervical smears. Furthermore, the popularity of medical topics with radio, television and the press has encouraged this demand to the point of straining current resources. In an attempt therefore to provide a more even coverage of all women it is now national policy to replace opportunistic screening with computerised call and recall. It is certainly true to say that all laboratories are doing more smears than they did formerly, but sadly it is equally true that the percentage of abnormal smears is also increasing. Several studies from around the UK echoed by reports from other countries have shown that the degree of cytological abnormality, especially when it is minor, does not reliably mirror the existing pathology. Hence more patients are being referred for colposcopy and diagnosis at an earlier stage in the disease process.

The circumstantial evidence is overwhelming for the Human Papilloma Virus (HPV) playing an important role in the aetiology of cervical cancer and its precursors. This sexually transmitted organism is common in the genital tract of both men and women. Indeed, it has recently been reported from a sample of the German population that HPV DNA has been found in the genital tract of 10–15% of both men and women. In the UK the incidence of genital warts has doubled over the last decade. The avoidance of barrier methods which oral contraception allows and wider public acceptance of casual sex have done nothing to halt the spread of the wart virus. Appreciation of the association between koilocytosis, the histological stigma of this virus, and cervical neoplasia has prompted a review of historical material and the constant coexistence of these lesions has been confirmed. HPV DNA has even been demonstrated in the HeLa cells so familiar to those involved with cell culture and which originated from a cervical cancer. It is hardly surprising therefore that the number of women in whom CIN is being diagnosed is now reaching epidemic proportions.

It must now be obvious to the most casual observer that the number of new cases far exceeds the number of invasive cases which could possibly be anticipated. Presumably therefore many patient infected with the papillomavirus have lesions which the body's natural defence mechanisms recognise and destroy. The lesion may be at a cellular level when this occurs, it may be a subclinical or clinical wart or it may be CIN of varying degree. Many, if not indeed most, cases of CIN 3 will not progress to invasive cancer. In the recently publicised New Zealand series, one third of the patients with untreated carcinoma *in situ* had developed invasive cancer within twenty years but two thirds had not. Currently, we are unable to predict which patients will develop progressive disease and which ones will not. Identifying the strain of virus involved may give us a clue as to the likely rate of progression, but the process is too impractical for routine use. We could simply choose to follow lesser degrees of abnormality in the hope of regression but the population with whom we are dealing tends to be mobile and may get lost to follow up while some lesions progress to invasive cancer in a surprisingly short time. Besides most women would prefer to have normal smears and be followed up rather than abnormal ones even when the abnormality is apparently a minor one. In practice therefore we are faced with treating all patients diagnosed as having a potentially pre-malignant condition.

The wart virus is known to be associated with the development of malignancy in other species and in humans is also associated with carcinoma of the vulva, vagina and penis as well as the larynx and anus. Malignancy does not develop at these other sites with anything approaching the frequency of cervical cancer. What makes the cervix different is the presence of a transformation zone and it is here that the cancer normally begins. Primary prevention of the disease might be achieved by lifelong abstinence from intercourse but in practical terms can at best be reduced to a minimum by lifelong mutual monogamy. Unfortunately in a country where one out of every three marriages ends in divorce this form of protection from cervical cancer is unlikely to bring about a significant reduction in numbers soon. Ironically, the attention given to the spread of the AIDS virus and its reduction by the use of condoms may similarly reduce the spread of the wart virus. What we can bring about is destruction or removal of the transformation zone of affected patients, with subsequent follow-up to confirm continuing cervical normality.

Initially, carcinoma *in situ* or what we would now call CIN 3 was treated by hysterectomy with at least some patients undergoing more radical surgery and/or radiotherapy. This was recognised as somewhat over-zealous and cone biopsy became increasingly popular, but the latter was still associated in some cases with the development of infertility or impaired cervical function in pregnancy. The fall in the modal age of patients with abnormal smears coincided with the introduction of colposcopy and this technique has allowed destruction of the transformation zone to take over from excision as the standard treatment.

Transformation zone ablation is normally achieved by extremes of heat or cold; it does not seem to matter how the cells are killed, only that they are killed. Dead cells do not divide. The ideal method of local destruction should be effective and safe, economical in capital outlay, maintenance and time, simple to use and highly acceptable to the ambulant patient preserving her fertility where desired. Let us therefore compare the various methods.

Patient factors

Effectiveness
In skilled hands destruction of CIN has been achieved in approximately 95% of patients regardless of the method employed. There is a theoretical advantage in achieving complete destruction of the lesion at the first attempt as the ground rules which govern the use of local destruction after colposcopically directed biopsy may be altered in a treated cervix. In other words, visualisation of the new squamocolumnar junction is not a virtual guarantee of normality above this junction.

Preservation of function
Again reports would indicate that failure to conceive, spontaneous miscarriage, premature labour, and cervical dystocia are no more common in patients treated with these various methods than in untreated women.

Pain
The application of either heat or cold to the cervix results in uterine contractions which the patient experiences as lower abdominal cramping. The degree of pain is probably similar with the various modalities with cryosurgery perhaps being the least painful. Historically we have imagined the pain from electrocoagulation diathermy to be sufficiently severe to warrant general anaesthesia while patients have been treated on a routine basis with both the laser and cold coagulator without any anaesthesia whatsoever.

Duration of treatment
This factor is intimately linked to the previous one since pain of any description is obviously far better tolerated if it is of a transient nature. In this respect the cold coagulator has a clear advantage since each application only lasts twenty seconds and most transformation zones would be destroyed in five overlapping applications. The laser is at a disadvantage here since it may produce troublesome bleeding delaying the completion of treatment. It is important to note that cryosurgery may require longer than formerly thought and that counting should not begin until the iceball has reached its desired size. The treatment of several patients in rapid succession with cryosurgery requires the use of a large reservoir if delay occasioned by a total freeze-up of the apparatus is to be avoided.

Post-operative discharge
Cryosurgery does have a clear disadvantage here since the killed tissue is not removed at the time of the procedure but remains to subsequently slough causing an offensive watery discharge which may persist for 1–2 weeks. The laser on the other hand has a clear advantage in vaporising all of the killed tissue except for a very thin margin of tissue subjected to thermal damage. There is therefore very little discharge after laser vaporisation. Some discharge is to be expected after both electrocoagulation diathermy and cold coagulation. In

any event, secondary infection of the cervix can be avoided by the nightly application of triple sulphonamide cream.

Bleeding
As already noted, intra-operative bleeding may be a problem with the laser. Post-operative bleeding is an uncommon event, but may be encountered with any of the methods.

Smoke—smell
Since there is no burning of tissue with either cyrosurgery or cold coagulation there is no smoke or smell, while these are the norm with both electrocoagulation diathermy and the laser.

Healing
The cervix treated by laser vaporisation will heal more quickly than that treated by either electrocoagulation diathermy or cold coagulation and the cervix treated by cryosurgery will only heal once the necrotic tissue has sloughed.

Economic factors

Outpatient use
Electrocoagulation diathermy is normally employed in the operating theatre under general anaesthetic whereas the other three methods are normally used in the outpatient clinic.

Capital cost
Every operating theatre already has an electrocoagulation diathermy unit and therefore this method has a clear advantage in that no new equipment is necessary. Laser on the other hand has a clear disadvantage, the capital cost being up to £1000 per watt. The standard carbon dioxide laser producing around 15–20 watts, the market is now witnessing the promotion of more powerful machines capable of 40, 50, 60 and up to 100 watts. Both cryosurgery and cold coagulation cost approximately £1000 per unit.

Maintenance cost
Again, being much more sophisticated the laser requires a much higher maintenance premium. Also the cost of a smoke extractor must be borne in mind for both electrocoagulation diathermy and the laser.

Portability
Both the cryosurgical and cold coagulation units are readily portable, the heaviest part of the cryosurgery is the gas reservoir but the gun itself can be carried in a briefcase. The complete cold coagulator unit weighs only 2.2 kg. The laser is capable of being moved along a level floor. Electrocoagulation

diathermy units may be similarly moved but many will be built into the operating theatre wall.

Other uses

Cryosurgery is sometimes used for treating haemorrhoids and genital warts have been treated with electrocoagulation diathermy and cryosurgery for many years. The precision of the laser comes into its own in this category since tiny warts can be readily vaporised and no other treatment can achieve the superficial vaporisation of affected skin in the recently described 'burning vulva' syndrome.

If these various factors are considered and equally weighted the cold coagulator emerges as the method of local destruction most closely approaching the ideal as defined earlier. However, the laser is undoubtedly the most popular method used today. In truth this is the result of its high-tech image. All other methods are mundane by comparison. The similarity between the various methods would suggest that where a centre possesses cryosurgery there is little advantage in purchasing a cold coagulator, and similarly where a cold coagulator is in routine use, there is little point in replacing it with a laser.

Concern has been expressed that the diagnosis of microinvasive carcinoma of the cervix is becoming less common and that undoubtedly patients with this condition are being treated unwittingly with destruction. This has resulted in a move back to cutting cones thereby providing the histopathologist with the whole specimen rather than representative colposcopically directed biopsies. The carbon dioxide laser has the advantage over other methods of destruction in that it can be used for cutting, but the greater power required means the use of more expensive machines. Yet another possibility is the return in a modified form of hot loop cones cut with a fine wire through which an electric current is passing. This new approach to cone biopsy has reduced the amount of time the patients spend in hospital. Many patients are treated as day cases or outpatients but even using the old technology of the simple scalpel it is still entirely feasible to deal with the patient as a day case. It is true that several papers have demonstrated that the blood loss with a laser cut cone is significantly less than with a knife but in fact the difference is not clinically significant and real advantages for alternative forms of cone biopsy have yet to be demonstrated.

Cervical intraepithelial neoplasia is obviously a testing ground for newer techniques as they appear. The Nd:Yag laser which works mainly by coagulation and less by vaporisation is currently under evaluation. Alternative approaches with drug therapy and immunotherapy will continue to be assayed. Nevertheless, the principle aim of the exercise must remain the prevention of invasive cancer of the cervix by detection and effective treatment of CIN and the technology to carry this out is already here and widely available. More than ninety per cent of women who develop invasive cancer of the cervix have never had a smear and our greatest opportunity for preventing invasive cervical cancer in the future is by the encouragement of uniform participation in cervical screening programmes.

DISCUSSION AND SYMPOSIUM SUMMARY

Dr D Jenkins
Consultant Histopathologist
Whittington Hospital, London

INTRODUCTION

Cervical neoplasia and its prevention is an important medical topic. It is also of immense and, at times, dominating public interest. The publicity and appetite for information in this field is out of all proportion to the modest contribution which cervical cancer makes to mortality, but is more justified by the frequency of potentially precancerous changes which in the most minor forms may affect up to 10% of the sexually active female population. A BBC producer explained this as, 'With sex elements the story can't fail'.

The cervical cancer story is a microcosm of modern medicine, containing all the scientific fascination and practical problems that comprise current health issues. There are the basic scientific problems of understanding the molecular and cellular pathology and the natural history of the development of cervical intraepithelial neoplasia (CIN) and its evolution to invasive cancer in a relatively small proportion of cases. There are the clinical problems of the selection, reproducibility, evaluation and organisation of the screening and diagnostic investigations and laboratory tests needed to establish a diagnosis of CIN, and the problem of the management of women identified as having mild cervical cytological abnormalities by repeat cytology or colposcopy with local destructive therapy, as well as the treatment of women with more serious disease. There is the human interest in a disease which can affect women from 14 years to beyond the menopause. Recent studies have highlighted the level of anxiety associated with abnormal smears, the lack of information given to patients and the difference in perception of smear abnormalities between experts and patients who can interpret a mildly abnormal smear as frank cancer.

Ultimately many aspects of the cervical cancer problem are political and ethical issues concerning decisions on the best use of resources and the greatest benefits to be obtained from different approaches, often having to make the decisions on the basis of partial and inadequate information. Politics is 'the art of the possible' and we must acknowledge the political component of a large scale medical activity such as cervical screening. Not since the days of Rudolph Virchow has a pathologist entered serious politics at a high level. He achieved success in the German Reichstag arguing with Bismarck in favour of liberal policies. How can an analysis of the present state of knowledge on cervical cancer help to assist current decision makers with regard to choices about research and practice in the prevention of cervical cancer and the management of cervical precancer?

THE PRESENT POSITION

There are three important themes which currently demand attention and which run through the whole story of cervical cancer. The first is understanding the cause and biology of cervical precancer and invasive cancer, and the relationship between them.

The second is the relationship of cytological abnormalities detected on screening to underlying disease. Much information on this which was not available when cytological screening was introduced has been provided from the widespread use of colposcopy in recent years. The accurate interpretation of much of this is not always obvious and has not always been as cautious as it should be, but nonetheless it does raise questions about the efficiency and appears to explain some of the failures of cytological follow-up of low-grade abnormalities.

The third is the implications of all these pieces of information for the design and organisation of screening programmes and the management of women with abnormal smears.

THE ROLE OF HPV IN THE MOLECULAR PATHOLOGY OF CERVICAL CANCER

In 1890 the understanding of the relationship of mycobacteria to tuberculosis was at a similar stage to the knowledge of the role of HPV in cervical cancer almost 100 years later. The German pathologist, Koch, determined that three postulates needed to be satisfied in order to establish a causal link between an organism and a disease:

1. The constant presence of the organism in every case of the disease

The frequency of detection of HPV depends on the sensitivity of the test used. Early studies using papilloma virus common antigen as a marker detected mature virus particles in about 40% of CIN, and about 12% of normal cervices.[1] Using Southern blotting the prevalence of HPV 16 was found to be 30–50% in CIN 1 rising to 80% in CIN 3, with a prevalence of HPV 16 of 90% in invasive cancer. Southern blotting also found a prevalence of 15–50% of HPV 16 in normal cervices.[2,3] The introduction of the polymerase chain reaction (PCR), which can detect a single papillomavirus DNA molecule in 10^5 cells, has suggested that the prevalence of cervical human papillomavirus infection at this level is of the order of 50–90% in women with normal smears[4]. It would appear therefore that an important difference is in the expression of human papillomavirus between normal women and those with CIN and invasive cancer rather than in simply its presence. HPV 16 is clearly expressed in different ways and to a different extent in the different groups. Much further study is needed before the significance of this is properly elucidated.

2. The preparation of a pure culture which can be maintained for repeated generations

Compliance with this criterion is perhaps the most difficult for HPV, but the development of methods for cloning HPV DNA in bacterial plasmids and subsequent transfection of tissue and organ cultures as described by Dr McCance and Dr Vousden largely answer this requirement.

3. Reproduction of the disease in animals by means of a pure culture

Dr Vousden has demonstrated how certain cell lines transfected with HPV 16 DNA or its component E6 and E7 reading frames can be transformed suggesting that this may have a role in tumorigenicity. Dr McCance has demonstrated the use of a system of culture of human foreskin keratinocytes which allows differentiation to take place and which when transfected with HPV 16 will produce changes which histologically resemble CIN, including cellular atypia, dedifferentiation and abnormal mitoses. The differentiation becomes less with progressive passage and changes of CIN 1, CIN 2 and of severe dysplasia seen in CIN 3 are found, although a true carcinoma in situ has yet to be seen, let alone invasive cancer.

There is thus considerable, but not complete compliance with Koch's postulates. HPV appears to be intimately associated with the evolution of CIN and experimentally HPV 16, at least, can transform cells towards a malignant phenotype. The involvement of HPV in the final stage of evolution of invasive cancer is much less clear. The ubiquity of HPV 16 suggests that, as with many other tumour viruses, the relation of the virus to malignancy is complex and many other factors may be involved.

The integration of HPV 16 viral DNA, and the expression of the control regions E6 and E7 may be important in the development of invasive cancer. Dr Tidy has indicated the role of maintenance and transcription of these reading frames continues into at least early invasive cancer. Other viruses such as herpes virus may play a role as cofactors. The role of other mutagens, of oncogenes, and of other somatic genetic changes in the evolution of cervical cancer is less clear, although the experimental evidence mentioned today of the involvement of RAS oncogene in fibroblast transformation in association with HPV 16 is very interesting. Intracellular repair mechanisms for DNA may also be important in counteracting the genetic damage.

The development of CIN and invasive disease takes place not only at the cellular level, but at the level of intercellular reactions. The local immune system is involved in the response to HPV and HPV infected cells and the Langerhans' cells may also be involved in epithelial organisation, the loss of which is a feature of CIN. Immunosuppression by cigarette smoke and by seminal plasma may be important, and HPV itself, especially HPV 16 and 18, also exerts an effect in reducing the local immune cell populations in the cervix. The increased tendency of immunocompromised women to develop cervical neoplasia suggests that the local immune response is important, but the disturbance of the local immune cell populations by factors such as smoking may also be a marker for other subtle effects on epithelial growth and differentiation. Other cofactors probably exist and may be important, for example, in China where carcinoma of the cervix is common yet smoking is uncommon.

A MODEL FOR THE RELATIONSHIP OF HPV AND CIN

Figure 1 shows a hypothetical model of the possible relationships between HPV infection of different types, precancer and cancer of the cervix. HPV is sexually transmitted and the demonstration of a high prevalence of male genital HPV lesions in the consorts of women with CIN may provide at least a partial basis for the 'high risk' male hypothesis.[5] The finding of small amounts of HPV by polymerase chain reaction in a majority of sexually active women suggests that infection with the organism is not uncommon. In the majority there are no detectable macroscopic or microscopic lesions, and it is possible that carriage of the virus is transient. There are no long term harmful effects.

In a minority of women visible lesions develop which can be detected by colposcopy. Most of the visible lesions are associated with only minor colposcopic and histological abnormalities. In these women the diagnostic histological changes of HPV infection may be very focal. The detection of these lesions by cytology is very variable and there is a high rate of false

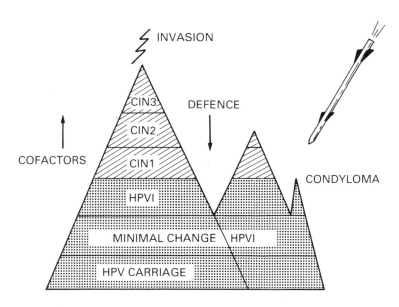

Figure 1. Diagrammatic representation of the relationships between the presence of HPV 6 and 16 and morphological disease in the cervix.

negative smears in this group. This makes it very difficult to interpret studies of the natural history of mild cervical abnormalities which rely on cytology.

A smaller proportion of women will develop the typical flat lesions of HPV infection seen with both HPV 6 and 16, and the condylomata associated with HPV 6. The relationship between flat HPV infection and CIN 1 is ill-defined and histological distinction is unreliable.[6] It is unclear whether there is a sharp biological distinction. Aneuploidy which is often used as a marker of malignant potential is a feature of some cases of apparently simple cervical HPV 16 infection as well as of CIN.[7]

Replication of HPV with a significant percentage of antigen positivity is a feature of both simple HPV and CIN 1 lesions as it is of CIN 2 also. Distinction between those lesions associated with HPV 6 or 16 is not possible by histology alone. Dr Barton has presented the evidence of a decrease in Langerhans' cells and T cells in these lesions, suggesting a local immune suppression, and cell turnover is increased.

A number of women with low grade CIN progress to CIN 3, others (possibly up to 40%) regress.[8] There is a high risk of women with CIN 3 and severe dyskaryosis (i.e. having a large enough CIN 3 lesion to yield adequate numbers of severely dyskaryotic cells to be detected by cytology) for the development of invasive cancer.[9]

Clearly at each stage in progression fewer and fewer women proceed towards malignancy. Biologically the evolution of malignant disease appears to be a multistage process; there is evidence for the involvement of HPV in at least some stages of this. Many important factors in determining the occurrence and rate of progression remain to be identified. The danger of women developing invasive disease while under follow-up and the serious ethical difficulties of studying the natural history of high grade CIN are illustrated by the New Zealand study.[9] The ethical impossibility of following the development of invasion has led to the use of CIN 3 as a surrogate endpoint in many studies, but this is not necessarily adequate for all purposes, and its uncritical use can lead to misleading conclusions, especially if the grade is taken as the sole gold standard and the volume of disease and other factors in the natural history are ignored.[10] The study of the natural history of CIN is also technically very difficult as invasive methods such as biopsy will destroy or considerably interfere with small early lesions, non-invasive methods like colposcopy and biopsy are not sufficiently accurate to predict fully the underlying histological abnormality. Without much elucidation of the process of progression, how many progress at each stage, why, and how fast proper planning of any prevention programme is, at best, inspired guesswork.

CYTOLOGICAL ABNORMALITIES AND UNDERLYING DISEASE

The cytological grades used in cytology screening were introduced at the time when there was a simple view of the relationship between smear abnormalities and underlying disease. Using current terminology the assumed relationships were: mild dyskaryosis implied CIN 1 lesions; moderate dyskaryosis, CIN 2;

and severe, CIN 3. Colposcopy has taught us that this is a gross oversimplification. Although severe dyskaryosis usually, but not always, implies CIN 3, moderate dyskaryosis is also very often associated with CIN 3, and mild dyskaryosis has, in many studies, been found to mask underlying CIN 3 in 25–30% of cases.[8,11] There clearly is more CIN 3 on colposcopic biopsy in women with lower grade smear abnormalities than was anticipated by conventional wisdom. The implications of this finding for the management of women with mild smear abnormalities are still being worked out.

The explanation for this discrepancy is complex and involves both methodological and biological factors which intervene between the cytological grading and the underlying disease[10] (Figure 2). In the method there are the collector of the smear whose skill is variable, the instrument used which may be one of several spatulae or brushes, the efficiency of the cytoscreener in detecting abnormal cells, the skill of the cytopathologist and the reproducibility of the cytological grading used, the skill of the colposcopist in detecting abnormality and selecting the most abnormal area for biopsy, and the reproducibility of the pathologist's assessment in applying the histological CIN grading. All these play a very important part in determining whether the smear report reflects accurately the underlying disease and contribute very substantially towards a false negative rate for cervical cytology of from 15–40% in

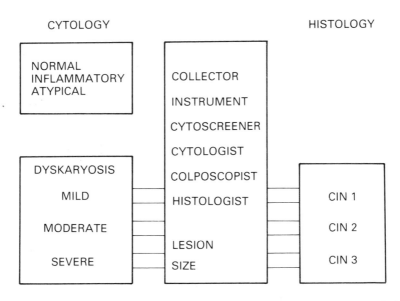

Figure 2. Factors influencing the relationship of cytological grade to underlying histological changes.

different studies. There is an urgent need to evaluate alternative methods of sampling the cervix, and particularly to discover ways of doing this which are robust enough to yield satisfactory smears when used by a variety of more or less skilled operators under less than ideal conditions. There is a need to ensure adequate training for all smear takers. In many laboratories up to 40% of smears may lack endocervical cells and may therefore not be fully adequate. External quality control is being introduced into cytology laboratories, but as yet has not been considered for colposcopists and histopathologists, although there is no evidence that their morphological judgements are superior. This needs to be linked to proper training and retraining of those who fail to meet satisfactory standards.

Proposed Model for development of CIN

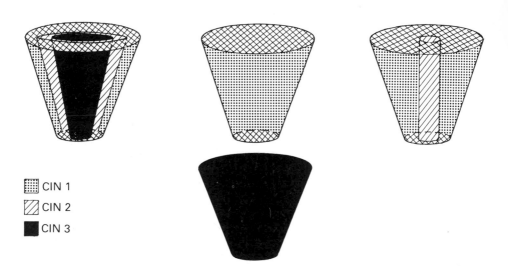

Figure 3. A diagrammatic three-dimensional reconstruction of the structure of CIN lesions.

Even when all these methodological factors are controlled there still remains a discrepancy between cytology and histological grade which can only be accounted for by a biological difference between lesions of the same grade which affects the cytological pick up of cells from the lesion. The size of a CIN lesion is important in this.[10] There is a clear relationship between the size of a lesion and its grade. High grade lesions are generally bigger overall than low grade lesions. This helps to explain why there are more false negatives with low grade lesions than with high grade lesions. The three-dimensional structure of CIN lesions is quite complex (Figure 3), especially for many CIN 2 and CIN 3

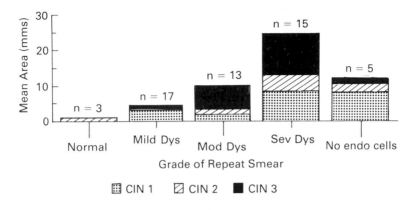

Correlation between Smear and Area of CIN

⊞ CIN 1   ▨ CIN 2   ■ CIN 3

Figure 4. The relationships of lesion size and grade to cytological grade.

lesions. In general CIN 1 lesions are small, although some can be large. CIN 2 lesions are larger overall but are usually composed of a large peripheral area of CIN 1 with a central small core of CIN 2. CIN 3 lesions are the largest of all. Some are purely CIN 3 and may be very large with extension of CIN deeply into crypts, but many consist of only a small central core of CIN 3 surrounded by CIN 2 and a wide rim of CIN 1, which may comprise the bulk of the lesion.

When lesion size is considered in relation to cytological grade on a spatula smear taken by a skilled operator under colposcopic control, one third of patients with mild dyskaryosis were found to have CIN 3. The area of CIN 3 in women with mild dyskaryosis was significantly and considerably smaller than that in women with severe dyskarysosis who had CIN 3 (Figure 4). The explanation is that women with mild dyskaryosis and CIN 3 lesions have a large surrounding area of CIN 1 which is sampled by the spatula, and only a small core of CIN 3. Women with severe dyskaryosis have mostly extensive CIN 3 which yields easily detectable numbers of severly abnormal cells. This finding demonstrates that there is an underlying biological group difference between women with mild dyskaryosis and CIN 3 and those with severe dyskaryosis and CIN 3. This size differential may well be important in explaining why women with mild dyskaryosis are apparently at a relatively low risk of developing invasive cancer compared to women with severe dyskaryosis even though CIN 3 is found on directed biopsy in a proportion of them.

71

CYTOLOGICAL SCREENING AND THE MANAGEMENT OF CERVICAL PRECANCER

The overall aim of all the current activity is the prevention of invasive cervical cancer by the detection and treatment of preinvasive disease. This involves three stage of activity: the detection of abnormality by screening which so far is achieved by cytological examination, the identification of those women requiring treatment which requires consideration of the cytological grade of the abnormality supplemented by colposcopy and biopsy, and the treatment itself which at present invariably involves destroying the involved area of the cervix, usually the transformation zone, in some way.

As Dr MacKenzie has indicated the organisation of a screening service requires the identification of a satisfactory programme for the detection of preinvasive disease based upon the natural history. In those countries where an efficient screening programme is established there is an apparent decrease in cervical cancer although it is possible that there may be other explanations for this than the effectiveness of screening and there is a general decline in the mortality of cancer of the cervix in the Western world even where screening is ineffective. In Britain mortality remains largely unchanged. Mr Singer has indicated that there is unlikely to be any major new developments in screening methods for the immediate future. It is not possible to be certain that cytological screening can reduce further the mortality of cervical cancer, but some women currently presenting with invasive disease have never had a smear. Others, however, have had negative or low-grade smear abnormalities. Careful audit of these failures of protection can help to target future developments. Improvements in mortality are likely to require both improvements in the logistics of the service and in the sampling techniques to ensure closer correlation between cytology and underlying disease.

The management of women with abnormal smears remains controversial. No treatment, even hysterectomy, offers complete protection for every woman. A proper decision on management policy demands weighing the relative risks of women managed by alternative methods for developing invasive cancer, and then an honest assessment of the cost-benefit ratio of each approach, upon which an ethical and political judgement can be made. At present there is insufficient information for a complete assessment of either of these for the current options: cytological follow-up, modified cytological follow-up, or destructive treatment.

It is generally accepted that women with severe dyskaryosis need colposcopy followed by destructive treatment of some form, whether hysterectomy, cone biopsy, laser therapy or cryosurgery. The options for treatment and some of the factors which need to be considered are discussed by Mr Duncan. Moderate dyskaryosis is probably best managed in the same way. The use of laser conisation and loop diathermy as discussed by Dr Anderson may represent an effective approach to these groups, but it is potentially demanding of histopathology services and the value of the additional information obtained about extent of disease in relation to the possibility of recurrence and the presence of microinvasion is uncertain. It needs to be evaluated.

The management of women with mild dyskaryosis is a very difficult question.[8,11,12] The apparent ability of an efficient system of cytological follow-up of women with mildly abnormal smears to, at least, partially control the development of invasive cancer needs to be reconciled with the high prevalence (25–35%) of CIN3 on colposcopic biopsy in women with mild dyskaryosis. The possible importance of lesion size in relation to this has already been alluded to. The study of Giles *et al.* presented at the British Society for Clinical Cytology in 1988 has shown that careful, colposcopically directed, multiple repeat cytology read by a consultant cytologist can accurately predict the grade of cytology in 95% of cases. This is an optimum performance, and is not achievable in current routine practice. A minimum requirement of very careful continued repeat cytology for mild dyskaryosis has been established and it seems very likely that this needs to be prolonged even if there are several normal smears if colposcopy is not to be performed.

Colposcopy for mild dyskaryosis followed by destructive treatment of any CIN found remains the ideal management, but has serious implications for resources. The importance of establishing a histological diagnosis in every case, and the best way of doing this remains uncertain. The possibility of a 'see and treat' policy is attractive, although whether all these lesions justify a laser cone biopsy and the attendant histological costs appears doubtful.

An intermediate approach using cervicography as a form of triage for women with mild dyskaryosis accompanied by a brush smear appears to produce an improvement over cytology alone. One major advantage of this approach, however, appears to lie in the provision of special clinics which ensure that a good quality smear is taken.

In the absence of controlled prospective trials there is no complete resolution of the problem of managing the woman with mild dyskaryosis. Preliminary results of a multicentre controlled study conducted from the Whittington Hospital suggest that there are slight but definite advantages for colposcopy over cytological follow up in the detection of CIN 3. The importance of this in preventing invasive cancer is not so clearly established.

Much of the discussion has centred on the effectiveness of the detection of CIN 3 by alternative methods. If the advantages of one or other of the alternative approaches are not that great the cost-benefit and the psychological acceptance of each alternative assumes great importance. Referral for colposcopy can generate enormous stress and cause psychosexual problems,[13] but prolonged cytological follow up is not necessarily free of anxiety. The patient's view and behaviour must not be overlooked in all this. Can stopping smoking or the use of condoms provide a form of prevention or delay the progression of CIN as the studies reported by Dr Barton and Mr Turner might suggest?

The complete solution to the problems of managing women with mild smear abnormalities remains to be found. There is certainly no shortage of work to be done in comparing the alternative options from a medical point of view and in developing understanding of the cause and biology of cervical cancer. This alone is not enough. A better understanding of the affected woman's point of

73

view and of her reactions is also essential to provide clear advice from the doctors to the politicians who ultimately decide the resources allocated to the prevention, treatment, and, not least, further research into this troublesome problem.

REFERENCES

1 Jenkins D, Tay S K, McCance D J. Histological and immunocytochemical study of cervical intraepithelial neoplasia (CIN) with associated HPV 6 and HPV 16 infections. *J Clin Pathol* 1986;**39**:1177–80.

2 Singer A, McCance D J. The wart virus and genital neoplasia: a casual or a causal association? *Br J Obstet Gynaecol* 1985;**92**:1083–5.

3 McCance D J, Campion M J, Clarkson P K *et al.* Prevalence of human papillomavirus type 16 DNA sequence in cervical intraepithelial neoplasia and invasive carcinoma of the cervix. *Br J Obstet Gynaecol* 1985;**92**:1101–5.

4 Young L S, Bevan I S, Johnson M A *et al.* The polymerase chain reaction: a new epidemiological tool for investigating cervical human papillomavirus infection. *Br Med J* 1989;**298**:14–8.

5 Campion M J, McCance D J, Mitchell H S *et al.* Subclinical penile human papillomavirus infection and dysplasia in consorts of women with cervical neoplasia. *Genitourin Med* 1988;**64**:90–0.

6 Robertson A J, Anderson J M, Beck J S *et al.* Observer variability in the histopathological reporting of cervical biopsies. *J Clin Pathol* 1989; **42**:231–8.

7 Watts K, Campion M J, Jenkins D *et al.* Quantitative DNA analysis of cervical human papilomavirus infection: a potentially malignant disease? *Brit Med J* 1987;**295**:1090–2.

8 Jordan J A. Minor degrees of cervical intraepithelial neoplasia. *Brit Med J* 1988;**297**:6.

9 McIndoe W, McLean M, Jones R, Mullins P R. The invasive potential of carcinoma in situ of the cervix. *Obstet Gynaecol* 1984;**64**:451–4.

10 Jarmulowicz M R, Jenkins D, Barton S E *et al.* Cytological status and lesion size: a further dimension in cervical intraepithelial neoplasia. *Br J Obstet Gynaecol* 1989 (in press).

11 Giles J A, Hudson E, Crow J *et al.* Colposcopic assessment of the accuracy of cervical cytology screening. *Br Med J* 1988;**296**:1099–102.

12 Robertson J H, Woodend B E, Crozier E H, Hutchinson J. Risk of cervical cancer associated with mild dyskaryosis. *Brit Med J* 1988;**297**:18–21.

13 Campion M J, Brown J R, McCance D J *et al.* Psychosexual trauma of an abnormal cervical smear. *Br J Obstet Gynaecol* 1988;**95**:175–81.

GENERAL DISCUSSION

Audience   If a lesion is destroyed locally, but after 3 months a repeat smear is positive, would you repeat the colposcopy procedure or proceed to a cone biopsy straight away?

Mr Duncan   We use cytology for follow-up. Patients who have an initial diagnosis of CIN 1 or 2 have smears at four monthly intervals for one year and thereafter return to the community to have a smear one year later, then every two years until the tenth anniversary of their treatment. Those with CIN 3 have an additional smear at 18 months and are followed in the community with annual smears between the 2nd and 10th anniversary. Regardless of the initial diagnosis all these women revert to normal screening frequency after ten years of follow-up.

If at any time their smears are abnormal, the same criteria for colposcopy are used as for primary referral i.e. colposcopy is offered with either a single Class 3, Class 4 or Class 5 smear. Two Class 2 smears would warrant colposcopy also. Cone biopsy would not be undertaken without first repeating colposcopy. Cone biopsy might be performed in the reassessment of the lesion, depending upon the smear report, the age of the patient and especially if the initial diagnosis was CIN 3.

Audience   What is the best way to manage a patient with a large abnormal aceto-white area on the cervix from which the biopsies are reported as HPV only, no CIN?

Mr Singer   If there is no CIN, I would leave it, but with HPV she is in a slightly higher risk group and I would review her in 18 months to 2 years. If she is under 20, I would review every 3 years. You might expect her to develop CIN. She will not return with invasion. In the past treatment of these cases has occurred too soon. A number of these cases are being found with cervicography. A prospective study is under way, in which the lesions are measured, reviewed annually, and compared with those being followed by colposcopy, over a 4 year period.

Mr Duncan   With such a big prospective study you must follow these patients and make sure they do not get lost. My philosophy would be simple. We just destroy the transformation zone and then review her and if the smear is normal with only HPV, she has a smear after a year, and if that is normal, she reverts to the normal screening frequency, because we have knocked out the target cells.

Audience   Mr Singer, what is done with the male partners of the patients with HPV?

Mr Singer   Men are a big problem. If a patient has more than two recurrences of CIN, we insist on seeing the male and then colposcope the penis. If the patient tells us that her male partner has warts, we advise her to get him to have

Tindall V R
Manchester

Tovey S J
London

Trowell F E
Ipswich

Turfitt M E
St Columb Major

Turfitt E N
St Columb Major

Turnbull L S
London

Van Dam P A
London

Varughese P S
Edgware

Venning C
London

Verzin J A
Belfast

Wade A A H
Leamington Spa

Walker S
London

Walzman M
Coventry

Wass D
Brighton

Webb J M
Berkhamsted

Welch J M
London

Wheatley Price M
Bristol

Whetmath B
Reading

Winceslaus S J
London

Wintle G
Lowestoft

Wisdom A R
London

Wiseman J F
Cambridge

Witt M J
Woodford Green

Wood L E P
Burton-on-Trent

Wotherspoon H G
Kidderminster

Wyldes M P
Leicester

MEDICAL RELATIONS PUBLICATIONS
CURRENT APPROACHES SERIES

Vertigo   (reprint October 1985)

Small Bowel Disease

Endometrial Carcinoma

Risk/Benefits of Antidepressants

Obesity

Affective Disorders in the Elderly

Childbirth as a Life Event

Sleep Disorders

Advances in Pancreatitis

Sudden Cardiac Death

Neuropsychiatric Aspects of AIDS

Stress, Immunity and Disease

The Problem of Recurrent Abdominal Pain

Breaking Bad News

Mental Retardation

The above publications can be obtained by writing to:
    DUPHAR MEDICAL RELATIONS
    Duphar Laboratories Limited
    West End
    Southampton
    SO3 3JD